MEMPHIS SHOALS

by Brad Crenshaw

BOOKS

Memphis Shoals 2022
Genealogies 2016
My Gargantuan Desire 2010

LIMITED EDITIONS

Propagandas 2012
Limits of Resurrection 1982

MEMPHIS SHOALS

BRAD CRENSHAW

Greenhouse Review Press

Copyright © 2022 by Brad Crenshaw

All rights reserved. No portion of this book may be reproduced or transmitted in any form or by any means, electronic or mechanical, including photocopying and recording, or by any information storage or retrieval system, without permission in writing from Greenhouse Review Press.

Published by
Greenhouse Review Press
3965 Bonny Doon Road
Santa Cruz, CA 95060

Design and layout by Gary Young

Cover: Harold Fisk, Ancient Courses, Mississippi River Meander Belt, Plate 22, Sheet 5, (Memphis), 1944.

ISBN: 978-0-9838094-5-6

Printed in the United States of America

for Brenda

Portions of this poem appeared in *Blue Islands, Blue as Ink*.

CONTENTS

Genealogy

Argument

15 The Saint of Vengeance

33 Revelations

59 Sirens

79 How the Widow Velma Learned To Dance

Genealogy

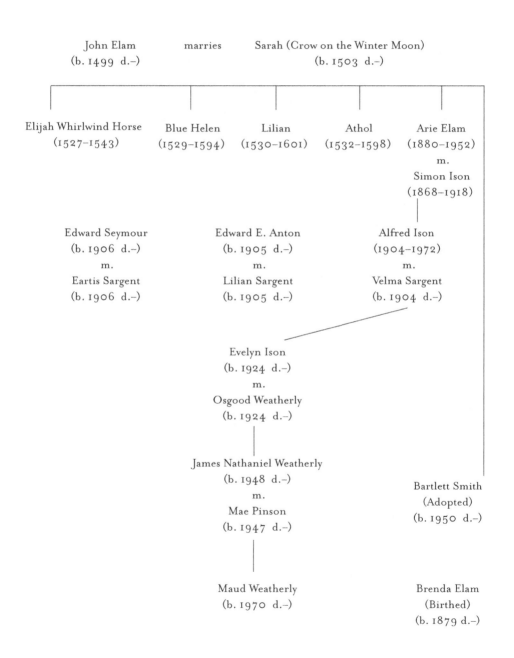

ARGUMENT

PREVIOUSLY, Alfred Ison was found dead and dismembered under painful circumstances. The events of his burial at the Memorial Park Funeral Home and Cemetery in Memphis, Tennessee, have been described in *Genealogies* by Bartlett Smith, one of the family members attending services. After the burial, the mourners returned to the home of Alfred's grandparents, John and Sarah Elam, for the last meal together of the reunited clan.

During the course of that evening, Bartlett related the curious history of John and Sarah, who are not of the modern world. Elam was born in 1499 in London; Sarah was born in 1503 to native tribes in Florida. Together, they traveled to Mexico to assassinate Cortés, and thereby change the course of history in the Americas. On their journey, they were lured into the sanctuary of ancient creatures winged like angels, fought against troops of militant spider-women, and at last, battled against the invading plague of measles decimating most of the New World. They failed to shoot Cortés, however.

Once returned to Florida, in 1521, they were accidentally rendered immortal, and spent the next 359 years pursuing what came to be known as genetic research, selling their advanced secrets to Gregor Mendel, who profited by the knowledge, and who has become deservedly famous. John Elam and Sarah have lived henceforth in secret, more-or-less, out of the public eye.

Bartlett took off for California after Alfred's burial in late July, 1972, but returned to Raleigh, unexpectedly, ten years later in June, 1982, for reasons he is about to explain to his two cousins, Ricky and Brian Haden, over dinner and drinks at Miss Polly's Soul City Cafe on Beale Street, Memphis. Today is July 22, 1982.

THE SAINT OF VENGEANCE

YEARS AGO you might have thought, as I
did once, faring among the farthest crowds
of islands, unbearably green, in Polynesia,
ringed with stone gods,
                                that I had dodged
ancestral prophesies, and finally
was shut of ghosts, momentous gossip and
the family doom, never to repair
again to Raleigh. I mean, I absolutely
thought I'd cleared my mind. For years I slept
beside the blue-eyed ocean, courting every
hour pouring over in the surf
among the agile muses on their boards
by day, and on the beach by night, by fires
beneath a wash of stars handsome in
the high air.
                So yeah, once you might
imagine I had lunged safely off
from my accomplishments and ends. My latest
lovely failure at the time had thrown
me out, amicably, and we had buried
Alfred, after all, in consecrated
ground. Also, everyone within
a year was silent once again, blessedly.
Elam reined back his offended blasts,
I made apologies for my mistakes
with Sarah,

                and eloped
exactly over burned bridges to
escape the facts and sad truths passing
for a way of life I thought was mine.
There wouldn't be for me any running
Southern judgment, as in the Bible, so
I'm grateful for my enemies. I made

Bartlett relates his adventures to his favorite cousins, Ricky and Brian Haden, who are his best friends in the family, though they may often fail each other as brothers.

The ancient Greeks believed the nine muses all were female, which suited Bartlett—for whom inspiration is erotic at its core, hence uncontrollable, intrusive, inconvenient, uncomfortable, and often tricky.

The consecrated part had been at risk.

In a sad, misguided variant of Sophoclean tragedy, Bartlett had taken an adopted son's liberty with his adoptive mother, which was not rewarded.

In this he's being dialectical, like Nietzsche, out of Hegel—and not really honest with himself or, therefore, with you.	my way to California, with its brimming coasts, its pools of disenchantment and regret,
	and those extravagant beliefs in earthly reinvention, promises
1982 is at the beginning of the AIDS epidemic in the United States.	of safe sex, not to mention transmigrating joys, as witnessed on the glistening beaches blanketed by actresses and beauties
This beautiful phenomenon can still be witnessed on L.A. beaches, and in Santa Monica, Malibu, sometimes Corona del Mar. By contrast, never in Long Beach.	browning in the sun of their ambition. Pelicans offshore would swoop for food on bent, pirate wings, while in the baseless air, gulls dropped like raucous angels tossed from grace. It takes me back, as if I never lived in sight of tricks, or missing
The homeless are close at hand, though sometimes hard to see when you don't want to look. We might bet they are the source of fear that informs our present cultural fascination with zombies.	persons rolled inside of plastic sacks. I was roused, and rough in my instruction, dazzled in the blue winds always in the way, rendering the far- away schooners blue at sea. They moved me like an errand in an unknown land, like promises, like rules I'd better try. So far, so good. Near at hand, drag queens were holding court in force against the less-gorgeous mortals put on earth
Proverbs, 17:22. Bartlett hasn't forgotten his Bible.	obscurely, whose broken spirits dried their bones. White men slept on graphic towels, and burned. Meanwhile, movie extras practiced unexpected love, and off around those fucking palm
On Muscle Beach on the south side of the Santa Monica Pier.	trees, quarterbacks kept making plays all day, and scored. Everyone auditioned as adults. On mats, amid the pandemonium,
To precess is to change according to precession, which is itself to alter the rotational axis of a spinning body.	were golden body builders lifting their eternal weights, and taking steroids sold by lab assistants winging frisbees onto precessed lyric vectors.

                    And well, yes,
since you asked, I was carried off
by whole cloth, and left not a rack
behind of Baptist trash, but worked on boats
holding melons, and manned the harbor tender
when I could, escorting visitors
to shore for tips. One time, late,
with weather coming in, I ferried to
a ship the size of dreams a shimmery, drunken
star bestrewn with jewels and ropes of pearls,
but minus shoes
                    —of whom was born, of course,
a famous trail of love, not unusual,
and who would later drown unfairly, I
should add, in another season, near
a Channel Island—
                    years, however, after
I politely heaved her lithesome body
into bed inside her reeling cabin,
feeling generous and grandiose,
as if I had new teeth. Whereupon
I lurched precipitously, pitched backwards,
and was thrown away entirely as
the schooner slued round, hugely, as
I heard it, in the mounting wind. I hurtled
like a lost comet, crashing on
a davit, while a deckhand madly slipped
the anchor, and we plunged away like horses
into foam and swell, with me in tow.

What may not be wonderful about
abstraction? what is this world? to be plucked
from one dimension, and deposited
with bruises innocently in some midget
cosmos run by half-deities,

> This was crazy, to go out in high weather. Bartlett was merely a deckhand on the tender, and so the decision was not his to risk the boat, and all on board.
>
> She drowned in 1981 near the coast of Santa Catalina. One conspiracy theory argued she was silenced by the CIA before she could reveal all she knew about the assassination of JFK. Another theory suggested that her husband pushed her over board.
> Also, sadly, she was intoxicated.
>
> To slip an anchor means to release the anchor and its chain from the windlass, thereby abandoning both to the seabed. This is a costly maneuver because you have lost both your equipment, and your capacity to anchor next time you want to.

As an aging king of England, Lear once enjoyed a related spectacle, whose thoughts were similarly affected. He had a pagan attitude, and welcomed the obliterating chance for vengeance.

Ocelots are commonly nocturnal, so Naomi was up running about at dusk, and during the night. When scenting their territory, ocelots squirt urine backwards, with admirable water pressure.

Insofar as the schooner had just weathered a violent squall, no one on the boat was interested in provoking anyone or anything into another storm. Just be cool.

Bartlett was an inconvenience. He had only the clothes he was wearing when he fell on board, as the schooner left. He had no place to bunk, no defined task, and ate like a starved horse from the finite stores onboard. So Naomi represented his chance for redemption.

half of whom were sickened by the yaw
and ocean roll engendered by Pacific
squalls—which usually are marvelous
when seen from land,
        but in their ardent midst,
I'm here to say, the morning blew its smokes
on board, and thunder followed close on thought-
executing fire, the sum of which
de-magnetized the common sense of Hollywood.
Someone brought an ocelot they called
Naomi, who escaped her cage, and once
the winds decayed a bit, the weather settled,
she would climb the masts, and slink along
the yard arms stalking sea birds as they roosted.
Lavishly, she pissed backwards in
the rigging, which appalled the yardmen when
they reefed sails that simply reeked of pheromones
designed to carry miles inside a jungle,
and arouse erotic promise, for
a price. A tactic old as war, if truth
be told about it. If truth pertains at all.
Honestly, you wouldn't either want
to risk inflaming the illiterate ocean
gods, a volatile lot by history,
nor rub the nether spirits up to rock
your bones with animal abandon, in
your wooden shelter, bobbing on the insubstantial
elements.

   And since, to some minds,
by closely defined reasoning, I was
a stowaway, and hoping to have all
charges dropped, I peaceably agreed
to clamber to the topsails, trailing strings
of bloody sausages, and lumps of steak,

with which to tempt Naomi to her cage.
On balance, little could be easier.
Conceding how I cut my teeth on Elam's
garden creatures—for instance, his invisible
snakes coiling in the basement, the winged
fish or something, plus the family wolves,
which were often vicious—, well, I wasn't
discommoded by an ocelot.
Aloft together, we were clearly without
secrets when Naomi leapt symmetrically
to the crosstrees, with her jungle eyes
lighting up the red meat I
extended. I made her reach across me, and
adeptly show her teeth to draw the ligament
of raw beef away. And so it was
I fed her appetites. She slipped into
my lap, her demon body purring like
a tractor, and licked the wisps of blood between
my fingers. I took her collar off, which let
her swallow,
         and from the main top watched the chief
navigational stars we followed spark
around me in the changeling darkness, vast
and starlit. Once I started getting cold,
I led Naomi down below for water—
where I peed into her litter box
to dominate her thoughts, should cats have thoughts,
such as they are. At heart, we both were built
from parts of blocks of sapience and feeling,
so it was alright. Naomi played like Rilke's
phantom in her cell, where I fed
her by hand, by the way, daily—
                  and to
the point, we neither one were disinvited
from the schooner once we sighted islands

The invisible snakes were especially a problem, and in the end all they could do was go down with the sort of fire extinguishers that use dry ice, and spray liberally around them to freeze everything alive. Then Elam stomped around to break the frozen snakes like glass figurines. The pieces were swept up with brooms, and dumped into the compost.

  Even so, an unknown number escaped into the wild to interbreed with native species, and for years afterward, the region was haunted by translucent pythons that ate the stray dogs, and an occasional sheep.

I don't know where he gets this stuff: Rilke wrote about a panther, not an ocelot.

The *Islas Marietas* are a collection of small islands outside of Puerto Vallarta, and are renowned for their beaches, and the snorkeling. They also are home for the blue-footed booby, made famous by James Tate—though he imagined them on the Galapagos Islands, where they also nest. They're birds: they get around.	off the blessed coast of Mexico: *Islas Marietas*, each about the size of any whale that breached around us. Pods of dolphin following, we ghosted to the gateway port. A motor launch collected our celebrities, and sped away to parties, and exotic matters prearranged by fame—which left the rest of us to shave, and draw our wages. The bosun promised he was going straight, and disappeared. I was given to the cook, who took
The cook was Don Otto, a kind man and mentor, though he had nothing to say about chickens. He said *chicas*, which Bartlett has misunderstood, given his insecure Spanish.	me off to market to replenish stores of ostrich meat, more beef, vanilla pods and chocolate, tons of onions, abalone in the shell—and who relentlessly was preaching. There were rules against stealing chickens, I remember. He was strung out on a man, and left me with the avocados, and my awful Spanish, while he looked him up, returning with a brilliant dancer, whom he introduced with loud, resounding empathy, as usual with him. They wandered way beyond their destiny, while I foresaw our market purchases on board, and stowed within our many-benched vessel—
His Spanish was improving.	though it was another year, another boat, and in another port before I understood the rules regarding
Black pearls were a natural industry in some of the remote lagoons of the Cook Islands, where the black-lipped oyster was native.	chickens. By then I'd beached in Polynesia: let's see, Cook Islands after pearls, and Samoa twice, where I sacrificed at shrines to the sea-goblins. I weathered older furies in New Zealand in

the winter rains, representing to
my mind a truly vengeful beauty. White
sharks struck at table scraps and butcher's
offal I tossed over for the spectacle.
Big-winged birds suspended in
the wind in my line of sight for miles.
Otherwise the latitudes were lonely—
bright, for sure, as every source of light
would scatter oceanic glitter, but we were on
our own. Below us rolled a rogue wave
now and then, exposing unexpected
wrecks, and drowned roots of islands. From
her golden throne, the moon-faced goddess watched
for small mistakes.

                Those who know about
my seamanship have said I'm upward man,
and downward fish, but I was unresigned.
Most cooks aren't lost at sea, maybe
one in ten some years, out in haunted
waters. Nonetheless, in Mexico
again, on land, when I was struck down
by treachery and shark ceviche, and shaken
empty,
        I was light-footed for
a month, pyretic, purged as angels—
about which I can fill you in on details
later dealing with denatured worms.
I took my leave from galley work, and lived
on broth, no smoked penguin, nothing
made of squid, no scallops, nor dishes out
of urchins, seaweed, sea bass, tentacles,
nothing to affront digestion. All said,
I was a model vegetarian,
purified within, and thought I'd try
a therapeutic gesture with the mutant

Bartlett surprised himself with an unexpected taste for Samoan foods, heavy on taro root, breadfruit, yams and bananas. Also turtle, but he pretty much skipped that one: the meat was too purple.

Measuring the height of a wave is uncertain as there is no stable referent. The largest wave ever surfed was proposed to be 100 feet high. The waves to which Bartlett refers are higher yet.

Milton said the same thing about John Elam.

Ceviche is a traditional Latin and South American dish made with chunks of raw fish marinated in lemon or lime juice. There are many variants. The pathogens in raw fish, however, include microbial hazards, and larger parasitic creatures.

Bartlett's love of vegetable soups began at this time.

women marvelously spread across
the beach, meaning no harm, but I never
got in range. I lacked words for what
I didn't feel about relationships
with strangers, even in utopia.
Knowing what I know, I wandered inland
after ocelots, and soon was hunting
caves, with bats like tiny demons squealing
from the core of solids all about
illegible truths and prophecies, reminding
me of home.

The power of telepathy requires constant focus, and mental will. A person's mind is organized by individual, organic structures that are not necessarily legible to an outsider looking in. For instance, think of the many different ways you might store your recollections of a cow: by color, by size, how they smell in a barn, as a food source, by economic indicators of milk produced, by images seen in Gary Larson jokes, as a source of methane— as well as by abstract scientific categories, such as *vertebrate*, or *mammal*. You might have an entire zoo, populated only by cows.

                I wish I saw that coming.
When I let her—if I ever was
receptive, Sarah with her painful psychic
sparkle clarified my shadows, and sometimes
planted hints that worked like bars of sun
illuminating features in the general
spreading plain of thought, which I would find
with emphasis inside my conscience. I
would hear a sighing door moving open,
and could smell her mental body on
the other side, out of sight, but emanating
tendrils of the native perfumed scent
of her, insinuating in the room
to root me to the spot, or tie me to
a kitchen chair with promises about
my life and after. I always felt her hands
were rough.
                Oh man. I brought all I had
away, dead or alive, and fled the cataclysm
moving me in Raleigh. Let the heart
of them rejoice who never have been wrecked
by sexual nature, wiped out, blasted,
never snagged by fascinating bait,

and axed. I was rattled. Those fluky noises
in the caves of Mexico were fishing
up subjective logic, and the catastrophic
urge to introduce myself to someone
else whom Sarah might have chosen.
So
I wrote to Laurie Brown, that saving friend
of hers in Oakland, if you'll recall, and claimed
to be clairvoyant: *I saw you bathing with*
an Indian, I wrote, *Maybe Creek.*
You gave her goodly words. I saw you blistered
in the living room, the carpet smoldering,
and also mentioned holes in gravity,
adding something with my Latin alphabet
about transcendence.

I had just returned
across a moving world, into the wild
islands rising violet, with fire birds
bombing from volcanoes, the green islands
ringed with stone gods staring, for all
I knew, into the source of meaning,
and here
I was in caves combining funky truth
with frank duplicity into illusions
square and formulaic, which duped us both.

Looking back, as if that helps, I meant
my best, which is roughly average when
it comes to bachelors seducing women
who, in Laurie's instance, measured happiness
by where she hurt. It's strange that pain should sing.
I had timed appearances, arriving
in her life around that period
of grief and longing after Sarah, with

When Sarah wanders among Bartlett's thoughts, her act is a feat of skillful exploration. Often, she introduced a conceptual architecture, in order to make sense of a foreign world. Think of Christopher Columbus, except womanly.

Sarah wasn't completely innocent in the transgressions between mother and son, but she was in control enough to retreat to distant boundaries at the last minute.

Bartlett, for his part, is lost. He was abandoned by one mother, and confused by the other.

Sarah teamed up with Elam in 1519, which, in the strange sequence of things, was after she met Laurie Brown in 1968. Thus in Oakland at the time of the Vietnam War, Elam remains in Sarah's future, and Laurie is in her past. Think of time as different places in space, and this makes sense.

Did you know that there are websites at which, if you are feeling scorned, you can plug in the name of the person whose fidelity you doubt, and there learn what other people have been saying about him, or her, or them? In this way we can all violate the privacy of just about anyone we choose to persecute.

These feral angels and centaurs are the *Araneidae* spider-women whom Elam and Sarah encountered during their journey into Mexico.

Everyone agreed in retrospect that Bartlett was unnatural to pursue relations with the early lover of his own adoptive mother.

Bogus research reveals that premarital sex breeds heartbreak.

her military heart, had launched herself
in flames into the afterlife—
                  leaving
Laurie charred and lonely in the living
room, as I said in code inside
my letter. Listen,
                I can explain it all:
how Sarah's camouflage was like the
saint of vengeance painted white, but dexterous
in bed. She was priced like a girl.
How Laurie was herself abandoned to
the future for an early English sailor
down the road, who foundered in his only
galleon, failed to even mate
with centaurs—or call them feral angels, I
don't care, he still bethought himself—, and later
shot Cortés, but missed.
                  We are novices
compared to Elam, *neophytes,* I told
her once we met, *babies* when it comes
to losing, which she maybe half-believed,
given her resentments and propensity
to cheat. She tired of every blessing, which simply
killed me over time, as if we never
had enough to eat, as if she drew
through my lips the insufficient sugars
of affection, and we starved.

                  I'm talking
years, of course, maybe three. We started
with the usual perplexities,
stoked at first, and dedicated to
the naked body of erotic work.
My. . . my. . . my memory
is fresh about our risks, and metamorphosis

as ocean people rolling in sensational
private waters, pinned in the coral beds,
a pearl of air ascending, and we caught.
Far from land, we'd surface gasping and
asphyxiated in the primal swell,
wild with what we'd done. She kept going under,
       which I misconstrued. *M'up,*
she'd mumble later, pushing me away.
She had to pee. At that time, when Josef
Mengele had drowned in other waters
where a frogman pulled him under toward
a coral fast, I abandoned boats
and magic travel, evaded fears of common
zombie jobs, and chose domestic orders.
I wrote code again for Pertec Industries,
deeply into banking. I'm good at this:
inventing languages,
          of which is born
intelligence itself inside machines,
which are called upon for blessings greater
yet than any other day of moving
money into tax accounts on islands
I avoided in my pirate time
on yachts. There were limits to my sympathy,
and other forms of battle. We rented an
apartment from a smoking melancholiac
with black lungs, who died a month into
our lease, and left a ghost behind alone
in the lower rooms. I wrote him notes about
the noise. Laurie heard him coughing on
the weekend nights, afraid of separation,
and enamored with our stabs at partnership
that over time elaborated into
quests for different colors in the kitchen,

Hypoxia had been known to increase the intensity of sexual experiences, which has in turn led to various erotic practices, sometimes ending in death. In 1936, in Japan, Sada Abe wound up killing her lover Kichizo Ishida, and was found days later carrying his penis and testicles in her handbag.

The frogman, according to Bartlett's yachting friends, was a Mossad agent operating clandestinely from a submarine off the coast of Brazil.

Pertec was a computer company in Irvine, California. Bartlett is excellent at what he does, and will attract government interest. In 2001 while messing around online, he will accidentally shut down the public telephone system in Belgium for 48 minutes.

The place was definitely haunted. No subsequent tenants ever stayed longer than 4 to 6 months, and eventually the building burned to ashes.

During a routine
exam, Laurie was told
she had a deformed
cervix, probably the
consequence of the
diethylstilbestrol
prescribed to
her mother to
reduce the risk of
miscarriage. The drug
actually increased
that risk, and also
caused congenital
malformations within
the reproductive
organs of the female
children who were
brought to term.

Laurie is working with
children who have
genetic mutations—
which, contrary to
the Marvel comic
imagination, are
almost always bad.
The Angelman
baby does not have
glorious wings with
which to fly, but
instead has intractable
seizures, intellectual
compromises, and
no speech.

One of the children
scooped an eye out
with a spoon. No one
saw it happen: one
moment she had both
eyes, and the next she
was missing one.

trips to therapists, visits with
her gynecologist about her cervix.
Laurie was incompetent, she said,
about conception, which was proven wrong
when we conceived.
                It was like, *whooff,*
it was like the inside of her head
combusted. She missed shifts at Project
Independence, where she kept the books,
and made mistakes. She listened. On the floor,
a Downs adult was pinching staff, and grounded
when he wanted to escape. The Angelman
baby started seizing. On the daily
log, she noticed that the little Smith-
Magenis creature went into the ICU
again. Autistic children rocked for hours
on the couches, screaming. Laurie hid
the silverware against self-injury,
noting that the same enemy
squatted inside her thought. By this pattern,
she internally evolved: helical chains
dissected, strange DNA was replicating
in her cavities. She vomited
for weeks.

        Looking back, as if that helps, even
after all these awful months, I was
transfixed in the dead hours in the bedroom,
where imaginary children drove
my sleep. On the nightship, I would tease
the swaddling babies without teeth, and fed
them daily. We lived in pumpkins. Toddlers bothered
no one. I loved it when the captain read
to us about our favorite autumn full
of parallels, when foxes brought the reddest

friendships in their hinged jaws. The weaving
spider shied away, inspired, and spinning
murals for the public good. In the virtuous
courts, mothers nursed their compliments.
How do you do? How do you do again?
Fathers began to grin. *You have her eyes,*
they told me, implying genealogies.
On the family tree, my heart hung
like a golden fruit.
                    Here is just
the moment, if I chose an altogether
average sample of the end of partnership,
I should select. Premonition woke
inside my frontal lobes the way extra-
large, non-moving fireflies flash
at night, out of nowhere, to disturb
my version of the peace. In the third
part of a minute, my dark narcotic eyes
pried open, and we bickered about
the carcass of our ardent plans. On
a planet full of accidents and bad
emotions, contrary wishes had miscarried,
one lie among so many, which
precipitated, in turn, by sad cascades,
a natural disaster dropping, in
the end, between her feet. Laurie walked
into an Oakland clinic known for its
discretion. From its mute rooms, she issued
with her loose and lustrous hair before
I was aware of absences—away
to Indiana and her ox-eyed mother,
queen of furies. *I've got it from here,* she said,
reportedly, inside my head—where
on the floor of thought, in their rags,
fringe women rose into an elemental

Most of us perhaps, love *Mother Goose*, but still reserve a distrust of foxes and spiders.

Bartlett could never reconstruct the conversation with a friend of his, also from Tennessee, about the compelling reach of sexual desire, in the middle of which, for no reason he could articulate, he suffered a crisis of perception. He later described the sensation of falling from a great height through the floors, in sequence, of a multi-storied building, until he came to rest in the basement, stunned amid the component facts of insight, and the debris of his illusions.

Never having had one, Bartlett is unclear regarding the actual accommodations of an abortion.

The Furies were often considered to be three female deities of vengeance: Alecto, Megaera, and Tisiphone. In Bartlett's instance, the three vengeful goddesses are Remorse, Guilt and Regret. Modern citizens have learned to torment themselves.

Her mother was a piece of work, and persuaded Laurie that, since she was home, she might as well have her nose fixed—the point of which was, I suppose, to improve her chances of getting pregnant again.

So he's 32 years old, and has grown skeptical about the laws of his own astonished heart.

He has arrived in Raleigh in June, 1982.

chorus, humming with Remorse, and Guilt,
long my favorite, sang like a murder
of crows among the black trees: *Days
of worry are at hand.* Regret came
in person with her acid breath, and blew
into my future.
            Oh, enough. Cousins,
that's all you need to know. Grief, the strong-
ass demon, peeled me like a grape. I'm
the age of Jesus when he saved the world,
raising up the good dead, according
to tradition, one of them. I've learned
I'm ready to repent. I did not
return to Raleigh,
            I *arrived* to reconcile
immortal mysteries with Elam and
eternal Sarah ageless in their grueling
comfort with the world, endless in
their history of love beginning over
after Mexico. I'm beginning over.

REVELATIONS

line of legal questions that arose
in company with probate law.
                          And so
it was I entered foster care the way
that Moses, in an empty lifeboat,
was blown into the reeds. An older, sterile
married couple from Biloxi took
me up, and fed me oyster spat to fatten
me until, astonishing all odds,
the wife produced, and they abandoned me
again to military care. Another
mother introduced me into her
neglect, a third became a Christian needing
someone she could discipline. Lorraine
arrived in time to serve me soup with croutons.
I recall Lorraine, tomato soup,
saltines and tuna melts. We practiced primal
screaming, which I recommend to any
masochist—one of whom we knew
was moved enough to show us to the Reverend
Moon. That was when Lorraine discovered
truth, and in a month was married in
a monster ceremony to a chosen
man in business selling hearing aids.
I was kept around as they recruited
other puzzled people, long enough
for Sarah to persuade herself, and Elam
to profess a future after all,
in a painful world, for biological
exuberance. I was nearly eight,
anxious and uneducated when
the social workers came again, brandishing
adoption papers full of Elam's promises,
and implying a suspicious Sarah's
treaty with devotion.

The concern here is who, if anyone, might turn up to make a claim upon their goods and property—and whether such a claim might have legal bearing.

A spat is a young oyster around a year old, and approximately one inch in shell length.

The reasons why families foster children remain various.

Primal screaming is a form of therapy, conceived by Arthur Janov, to address the psychic distress of childhood trauma by reenacting specific incidents in order to express the unconscious, repressed pain. Unlike talking therapy, these sessions are loud.

The Reverend Moon was in favor of marriage, and arranged them between eligible men and women, who were then married en masse in a large public event.

Technically, it is uncertain whether the spider-women were in Mexico, but Cortés was there, and so was Sarah when she was shot.

The one exception seems to be *them*, though it wasn't yet the case—and this is assuming a rather limited concept of death, omitting the death of stars, for instance, the collapse of the universe.

I'm hearing Verdi in all this wind, not even distantly, like the *Overture to Otello*.
  For the fun of it, you might check out the Sydney-Hobart yacht race just for the images.

                So, in another
way, Elam's revelations on
that unexpected hour given in
a string of days within the circuit of
our history, was less about my covert
parents, than about proliferation
filling up the vessel of the universe
with children, proper heirs, and populations
of survivors arriving after shipwreck
in a world returned to laughter. After
Mexico and their disasters with
Cortés, the plague of measles, spider-women,
and that rifle wound to Sarah's pride,
beware of saying anything about
affliction, or blame. Lately, I'm embarrassed.
Elam is an expert, Sarah is
a veteran of violent life, and both
are disciplined by hollow death hotly
in pursuit of every claim ever
made upon legitimate vitality.
From the start, they're lovers on a boat
with black sails and flags. They made away
after Mexico, as mountainous swells,
white-capped, arrived by destiny
to swamp their souls. Floating over the open
gulf below them, Elam ferried Sarah
wildly on the bright sea, sailing
out of infamy on wild winds
befouling all their enemies, blowing
ships like toys into the wave-washed
islands. Think about it. Fear was steady,
stress momentous in the salt wastes
and great waves of ocean, weird all
the way down, where water serpents wait
in deep patience, and whales descend in pods

through the blue rooms, singing of
the surface world. If you add it up,
Elam sailed his best. He said himself
it wasn't much, but he ran beside
the running god of luck—and thus the storm
and thunders were a shield against corsairs,
armadas on maneuvers, random privateers
firing flaming cannons. They were imperiled
and in pain, but made it, barely, as
a team, one thick, steamy evening in
a mist, the moon wrecked up there somewhere
as they reached the shelving beaches and
escape in Sarah's native glamour.
                                                At last,
they napped, once they were up to it,
dozing afterward, and while they rested,
drowsed some until they tired, the night
so quiet as they rolled together in
their hammock into headlong sleep, totally
conked, until the white and rising day
retrieved anxieties. He bandaged up
her bullet wounds, don't think she's
forgotten, her heart floating free. She listened
to him listen to her breathing in
relief among the noises made by jungles.
I'm good, she wheezed, considering she hadn't
eaten while the terrifying gale
of safety sank opposing navies as
it blasted her and Elam on the superficial
molecules across the world, especially
the liquid parts that freaked her out. They boiled
the last iguana for an incomparable meal
of greenish, stringy meat they each threw
in chunks into their thrown-open mouths
with a conviction, and the abject honesty

Cuba was an active staging ground in the 16th Century for expeditions—both military and private ventures. So the waters of the Gulf of Mexico were frequently populated by sailing ships.

This was, of course, before Florida was over-developed, and sinking once again into the primordial ocean—which is rising to reclaim its own.

Whereas the saltwater may have helped her heal up, the incipient scurvy would have prevented collagen maintenance of her scar tissue, re-opening old wounds.

The average depth of the Gulf of Mexico is 5299 feet. Their cutter had a draft of roughly 7 feet. So they were sailing over the superficial top 0.1321% of the ocean.

That is, Spring 1522.

No one in the family
ever returned to the
sea, until Bartlett
himself sailed away
into his future, and
Sarah's past.
  Sarah and Elam
settled in, and never
journeyed much over
sea, or land either.
They left Florida
in 1700, after 179
years of solitude,
and meandered into
Tennessee, where
they remained until
events in 1982, when
they relocated to
California. *See below.*

They struggled to
accept the depth of
their failures, given
the consequences to
the shape of Western
civilization.

Sacagawea, for
instance, was pregnant
with her first child
by the age of 14. She
died at the age of 24.

That is, 1543.

of their privation. When April came, relenting
in the winter fasts, and finding emphasis
on different goodness, and other forces, they
had come upon no rival to iguana
meat for triggering traumatic grace
and thanksgiving. At that time, they were in place
away from water: no lakes or basins, oceans,
seas or gulfs, no surf, waves or swells.
No superfluous lust for an adventure
tempted anyone—excepting maybe
Elam in his forty years of martial
wandering. I'll come to that.
                    In sum,
by magic or by miracle, they sailed
away from revelation, injury
and bloody dread. But if they celebrated,
if they were safe, I really couldn't say,
for they had thoughts. They did. How worlds
do end. The quaint gears of the
apocalypse had red teeth meshing
in the synchrony of catastrophic
meaning, which they never did accept.
Seven years they suffered from the demons
of perplexity, huddled in
their hidden village. What now? Chronologically,
and in the lateness of fertility
at twenty-three, Sarah started
on her pregnancies—like Eve afterwards
with Adam, you might think. Like rabbits, actually,
in the plain correction of biology,
once she wasn't starving, or in shock—
though not, strictly speaking, wholly willing
or prepared. Elijah was a whirlwind
before he sickened in his latency,
and died among his siblings in his teens,

elicited best joys. Drawn
down the years, she stood in fascination
at the gate of secrets, and in sight
of revelation, jubilant at even
minor congress with the miracles,
magic beasts and people about in the world.
She was not going on forgettably
through her day, full of family
and dreams. A prodigy herself, she gaped
at the prodigious Elam—there enveloped
in his ritual contrition, which
was on her nerves already, shy and angry
as she was, and just about to brain
him with a rock,

                when Lillian preempted
her in unkind heat, stabbing with
the fiery swords of blame and accusation,
using broad scarring strokes, and she
was rolling toward a diatribe about
abandonment, about vile old
age, wretched in both, when Helen fell
like wild-looking weather with her sightless
eyes rolling, calling *Athol, don't
leave me comfortless,* who brewed her herbal
remedies for pain, and inner vision.

For the record, Elam wept for seven
days, and never purged the last of his
regret. His life was made from war and sound,
such as it was, or had been, chiefly war,
into which, with his permission, incrementally,
Sarah mixed the kind euphoria
of their communion and permissible
desire. He listened. About a variety
of small matters Helen wove from darkness

Sarah was home raising their family while Elam was off on his gratuitous raids, regarding which she was not wholly sympathetic—though she was not sympathetic either with the European invasion of the New World. It is safe to say that neither she nor Elam was entirely happy.

A feature of Lillian's mental health is the ease with which she mobilizes her anger.

A feature of Helen's mental status is her vulnerability to anxieties, which arise because she cannot see. That she has lost her sight is precisely one of the reasons she can construe threats in the world. She has been bereft of something precious.

Research suggests that here is one of the first historical instances in which an adult white male respected the wisdom of an adult non-white female. Such respect remains uncommon among those territories now dubbed the 'red' states in what is mistakenly called the American heartland.

You may be pleased to know that science, to calculate the strength of an antidepressant, will construct a large, clear tank in which a small, clear platform is glued. The tank is then filled with water exactly to the top of that platform. A rat is tossed in the water, and the length of time is measured during which it swims, hunting for that invisible platform until it gives up in exhaustion, and allows itself to drown. The longer it swims, the better the antidepressant. That, at least, is the theory.

White willows are rich in salicylate acid, a potent blood thinner, and the primary active ingredient in aspirin.

her illuminated record of
the steps of reconciliation, starting
with the time when Athol gave his formula
for curing sadness, and restoring hope.
The fault is in ourselves, he claimed, and ladled
serotonin agents into subjects
Lillian recruited under Elam's
tutelage—then incontinently
tossed them howling in the swirling river,
measuring how long they took to save
themselves unaided. Or Elam fished them out,
mad as bats. By and by, they understood
the potion failed to fix despair, no
disposition ever lifted, no life
emancipated from genetical
restraints and finite strength: the ancient practice
of mortality remained opaque.

                I send
my love across the quantum channels of
the family to bathe the heartsore, early
members of the clan with admiration
and respect, as they addressed their grief
to the mysterious mess of puzzles they
were dedicated to define. The sweet
redress of labors in their laboratory
gave to Helen extra years of doubt
when they distilled a bitter broth from white
willow bark to thin her circulation,
and prolong her kidneys. She died, of course,
resigned to her subtraction from the sighted
world she'd half-deserted anyway,
which ruffled Athol's strength of mind, and left
him inconsolable. A childless man,
he carried on a while,

                    as when a nomad
angles for his last oasis in
the wasteland, going to his rest. He went
to sleep as usual in darkness, and reappeared
one morning in another state of being,   Sleeping can be
through no effort of his own—as when   dangerous. It is not a
                                                          benign kingdom at all
you see Pacific winds arising out   to enter.
of nowhere, stirring currents, the atom of
their animation powering fleets of sails   This phenomenon
and motion on the visible ocean surface,   is observed famously
                                                          along the low-pressure
until they cease inexplicably   areas around the
to breathe, and inspiration stops. Everything   equator. Bartlett has
is lost to this great decay. Elam   sailed through them.
                                                          Elam never reached
carried out his corpse, which Sarah washed,   that far south.
and dressed again in buckskin, adding precious
beads. Once more no man or woman flinched   The funeral custom
in the assembly of village elders,   herein described
                                                          disguises the nature
brothers, and the well-dressed wives of friends   of the situation with
of friends. Shamans came from neighboring camps,   festivities and a wall
following the old feeling of   of sound—thereby
the nursling guilds of trumpeters hitting   confusing evil spirit-
                                                          creatures, who may
the infrasonic phantom tones of God.   be on the prowl for
Idiophones wailed, the flautists were mostly right,   vulnerable souls.
sliding up the pentatonic scales,
and children hammered at the drums with brandished
antlers. Everyone processed behind
the family, all escorting Athol
to the grave and burial, returning
afterward into the palace of
the Elams' yurt to feast on smoked meats
and yams. Lillian was cruel in
her eulogy, and with blasphemous energies
resumed her work among the mist-enshrouded
fields of toxic foxglove and ephedra,   Both plants affect heart
which she used to touch her heart—that leaden   rate, and heart rhythm.

> A phytochemical is any compound found in plants that is bioactive—such as digoxin, found in the foxglove. Lillian and Elam are hunting for those that actively influence cell regeneration.
>
> Elam, to his infinite grief, never told her so, and upon her death cut off a finger in his chaotic distress, but it re-grew.
>
> She was on her way to creating Cerulean warblers by using grafts, which Elam managed to perfect without her, years later in Tennessee.
>
> Lillian was surprised to find the one thing in her life for which she thought it worth losing everything.
>
> In physics, entropy has been proposed to explain why time appears to move only in the one forward direction, when there is nothing in the math itself that would assign a trend or trajectory.

vessel with its virgin love intact.
She harvested the earth for sympathies,
appearing as she always did with Elam,
searching for the sorcery and signs
of phytochemicals that might regenerate
a life, and light it up divinely with
sufficient time to play among the truths
of being. I like to think she knew, no
matter what, she was a muse to Elam in
her final years of otherworldly work
with grafts. When she collapsed, gasping in
the seed heads of her latest livid grasses,
Elam thought *she's come back from worse—*
regarding which, be it for him, or be
it for Sarah, Lillian was far from her
return. Her vascular beds opened. She
believed her enemy was sleeping, but
the Devil was in love, grinning like
a shark, and tempted her with unequivocal
principles
        —regarding which, despite
everything that happened later in
their garden nursery, and even Tennessee
with timber wolves descending out of fuchsias,
and bears emerging as expected from
the mutant sundews, Elam never would
have given her the absolutes she found
without him. She left where she was living, and
abandoned Elam to his time with Sarah,
in the lonely paradise of mindless,
biological proliferation
hauling them by entropy into
the sluggish, daily, tedious crawl between
the final moment of her burial,
and the absurdly violent century

of holocausts we're currently inhabiting,
on the coast of foreign war. They
weren't born for this. Long ago they settled
scores with armies, public executions,
traumas and revenge, and even flew
above their worries on occasion—above
the cosmic probabilities, vested
in their merry animal fire,
        and in
the invisible world of form. Many years
were spent at their inventive and experimental
reptile flowers, continuing a line
of research Lillian detested, which
eventually they abandoned for
the famous century of birds and body
parts manipulated out of grafts
of hybrid dicots and their allies. It pleased
them to perfect the magisterium
of mammal vegetations, growing bears
and revelation wolves,
       until the time
of life in Raleigh, in their nursery,
when the reconstructed peace was tested
by a purely earthly glory blowing
through in that July. Thunderous weather
had arrived, tornadic winds were rising
by them, pulling loose the window panes
to suck their symbiotic cuttings into
emptiness, obliterate their vegetable
pigs, and every pilot bed of prototypes,
total ruination, brainflowers
seizing on their stems. Lightning fried
the wiring.
    While Elam rigged the storm
lamps, Sarah with her hair alive

These were hard years between 1601 (her burial) and 1982 (the current moment in a violent century), with those mutant wolves roaming up and down the inhabited valley. They changed the wild ecology of Western Tennessee and Kentucky until the New Madrid earthquakes in 1811–1812, which abruptly created new landforms, including Reelfoot Lake, when the Mississippi River ran backwards.

A dicot is one of the two groups of flowering plants, in which is contained most garden plants, shrubs, trees, vegetables and flowering plants. Hollyhocks are dicots, for instance.

That is, life in July, 1880.

Tornadoes often tear up the lower Ohio Valley. On April 3, 1974, 148 tornadoes erupted to kill over 300 people. Some survivors claimed the destruction was a sign of righteous judgment, and even the impious multitudes agreed it certainly felt that way.

A hemiparasitic plant obtains some of its nutrition from a host plant, and some from its own photosynthesis. *Rafflesia* is the genus of the parasitic corpse flower, which is also the world's largest bloom, measuring 3.5 feet across, and weighing 24 pounds. It smells like rotting meat. Twenty-four pounds of it in the open sun. Horizontal evolution is a process by which genes are shared between different species, and not passed down vertically to an offspring from its ancestor.

When the pod dissects along its seams, the tissues are separating in the way that, years ago, a stylish woman might snag her panty hose to start a run in its sheer woven fabric.

This poisonous hair is an evolved form of lanugo, which is often produced by fetal hair follicles during the second trimester to keep the baby warm inside the womb. They may also serve to protect against predation.

and writhing watched an ion bath infuse
the room to animate the hemiparasitic
fruit that she and Elam sequenced from
Rafflesia, or some other awful genus,
in an act of horizontal evolution,
sharing genes.
                 The nursery was trashed,
it didn't matter, vast cascades of glass,
the pump fused, blue flames lit
the chimney, flickered cool along the roof
trees—but everything unseen, nothing
even noticed save the green enormity
they had created, basically hominid,
as in a new family, only
green, and swimming in hormonal fluids.
Elam rent the amnion before
she drowned, and with the pruning shears cut
the long umbilicus involving like
a pumpkin vine. Along its seams, the pod
dissected on its own, so Sarah, reaching
in, retrieved the baby who, I have
to say, based on ESP and strong
presentiment, of which I don't approve,
usually, was unexpected, and overspread
with nettle or a fell of toxic hair
that brought a rash of blisters out on Sarah's
arms, which, hopefully, didn't hurt.
Thunder surged, red combustion rained
on them when hail and sulphur winged through
the shattered roof, inducing them to shoot
like stars and comets to the underworld
of shelter in the basement. Elam weighed
the baby on the scales he used for tissue
samples after amputations, as was
his way, wholly vexing Sarah who,

I like to think, as she opened up
her blouse, her breasts spilling out delighting
Elam, drew from brute humanities
to give her nipple to the artificial
girl that she retrieved forthwith from scientific
measurement, noting her immortal
constitution had already overcome
the allergens defending by design
the alien baby from predations, mortal
hazards, mutability, and psychic
enemies who get too close.

> He and Sarah had been developing xenografts from his vegetable pigs, in the course of which, amputations and other surgeries were requisite. The incentives for these grafts arose when Sarah, once, in tending to an infant burning up with measles, flayed her alive by unwrapping her swaddling, to which her oozing scabs had dried.

                Intuition
prodded her to think of *Brenda* from
the Norse word for swords. I know, right?
Brenda's so lame to call that combination
golem and adult divinity
I later saw on tape tempting lions,
and here seducing Sarah into ancient
motherhood again against her nature,
off and on abused by sorcery.
Nonetheless, it's Brenda suckling at Sarah's
breast inducing milk, and Sarah's skin
protecting Brenda as she rests, and puts
herself together in developmental
chains of steps of cell migrations, long
bone growth, the orchestrated helices
of DNA that fold in shapes like mothers,
metaphorically considered, bringing
rain to their families, probably
more so. Her auxiliary hair
was shed in baleful clumps, which possibly
destroyed the house cats, and though I haven't
mentioned it, as she faded over
weeks from forest green to sea blue

> Brenda, however aptly named, is later seen on tape (July, 1982) at Alfred Ison's funeral (July, 1972) throwing apples at the lion plants. See below in *How the Widow Velma Learned to Dance*.

> Even among non-nursing women, lactation can be induced by allowing the infant to suckle, which will stimulate milk production.

> Their house cats had a hard life, since they were often eaten by the garden beasts, or poisoned by the hemotoxic plants.

Sarah was in her own mind unsure about the virtues of this change, and preferred Brenda in her early sea-blue-to-pink phase, which for a while combined into a lovely color purple.

People have often been known to enjoy holding on to grudges—which, after the Civil War, became a major and continuing cultural pleasure identified in certain social circles as *Weird White People Shit*.

The process that rendered Sarah immortal did not provide her with an infinite number of ova. That she became pregnant now was the accident of a random stem cell maturing into a gamete, perhaps influenced by her delight in the infant Brenda.

Ancius Boethius was a Roman senator in the early 6th Century, who wrote *The Consolation of Philosophy* while in prison awaiting his execution.

Elam was inclined to Platonism.

to blue and soon to bluish human pink—
in the sequence of hematic bruising—,
Elam was relieved that he might creditably
stroll outside with Brenda in his arms
into the violent and inbred countryside
of veterans surviving Shiloh, who were
intemperate in general regarding
racial color, and had kept their guns.
On such occasions, meaning as he walked,
he sometimes thought that, if provoked, he would
reprise his military marksmanship
and shoot in secret euthanasia every
stupid life form wearing grey.
That must be his cure. He had a rifle
of his own, which he couldn't use,
which you know about, which is water
under the bridge.
          On such a morning, under
no compunction whatsoever to
curtail unfevered happiness in drifting
through their primal gardens showing Brenda
to apprentice spirits in the making,
Sarah said to Elam that he said,
once upon a time, that she could say
almost anything musically,
and told him she was pregnant.
          It's true that Elam
rarely thought about Boethius,
although he shared the same respect for consolations,
plus he thought philosophy was pure
genius, it drew off his darkness,
so he laughed at first, softly, sort
of, then he lost it, howling like a loud
and wolfish lunatic, which infected
Sarah in a minute with unbearable

mirth—two transported beings in
the beds of bursting poppies, screaming at
the vagaries of fucking reproduction,
whoooo, I mean, after centuries
of firing blanks, so to speak. *Heh.*
Around them pulmonary shrubs inhaled
with an amusing air, and set them off
again: they woke the baby. Veinous orchids
pulsed.

> Those centuries extended specifically between 1532 (the birth of Athol), and 1880 (the birth of Arie). Three hundred forty-eight years.

      So things go with those of us
with no regrets or discontents, chirpy
all the time, constantly, no
grievance with the cow-eyed beauties
of biology and their genetic train
of logic orienting everyone
to temporalities, and the communion
on the blue train of sorrows with
maternal love and mortal pain, and miles
and miles to cover. Not me.
                            But they
were like balloonists high on natural
buoyant principles, and floated through
the months of pregnancy when Sarah turned
in her circumference like a sun, her whole
creation open, by the way, a chapel
open to its goddess growing limb
over limb within the private place
of worship, and searching over time through Sarah's
entrails, stirring her torpid liver, compressing
her intestines with an active love
so vital and dependent that the beauty
of it gave no peace. Eventually
it seemed too dangerous to carry on,
she would rather not, at least—and yet
as she will tell you, once her water broke

> You might speak with Linda Maria Ronstadt about this genus of sorrow, of which she is a great and enduring authority.

> In Sarah's aesthetics, Ideal Beauty does not feature personal comfort.

Trilobites are arthropods that first appeared in the early Cambrian period, and were wiped out in the mass extinction of the Permian eon.
  Sponges are an even older animal phylum.

and scalded Elam's arms with prehistoric
broth that smelled of trilobites and sponges
from primordial bogs, her delivery
was fast. *Whoa! whoa whoa Whoa!*
were Elam's famous words commemorating
Arie's slide into his nifty hands,
as great as any, and full of atoms as
he caught her in this wretched world the way
he caught a mermaid once. Gingerly,

Let's admire Elam's prudence, which is widespread and open even to impractical threats.

just in case, he cast his charm against
untimely drowning in the barren sea,
the smoking breakers thundering.
      Sometimes
I really wish I thought like heroes and English
paranoids, but, well, nope.
With his words he handed Arie over
to her mother with the gleaming eyes
who, exactly unlike Elam, swam
through endocrine cascades to reach an island
of hormonal bliss, and there, avoiding
every shark of grief, forgave us all.
She didn't crash—that is, I think she stayed
awake, and wasn't weirded out by hemorrhages,
which was just as well. The afterbirth
was gross, but over. Elam felt around

A fistula is a separation in the birth canal that sometimes occurs during obstructed labor. Sarah was unaffected.

for fistulas,
    as morning with its rose
fingers woke the great convexity
of dreamers. At that time, his mind astonished
in its pond of guilt, he finally
remembered Brenda, left untended in
her crib in the wilderness, from whence she had
escaped. Crawling on her own on hands
and knees into his court of plants, she ate
the seeds of his experimental megabats

and flying squid, neither poisonous,
plus a carpet tack that passed undigested
through her plumbing.

> He knew what she ate because he carefully sifted through her scat, which she had deposited everywhere.

                      You might rightly wonder
whether Elam's rule thereafter with
his gardens—well, those remaining after
devastation visited with mortal
cyclones—whether, I'm saying, *listen* to me,
whether he retired his curiosity
and fear, forsook his science, just to parent
ornaments, to shelter fortunes in
the world, namely, Brenda with her naked
fate, and Arie always second and
forever practical.

> The question has been present in Bartlett's mind for some time why Elam and Sarah stopped practicing their version of science in 1880, the answer to which has multiple threads. His inquiry has been self-interested, founded on his essential disappointments.

                    But he'd been selling
secrets and genetic mysteries
to Gregor Mendel and his monastery
since the siege of Memphis, when he smuggled
feral seeds and unknown spores inside
the minor *Book of Jonah* inside Bibles,
mailed religiously to agents of
St. Thomas Abbey, who in turn delivered
holy relics hiding morphine jellies,
early sulfa drugs, bone saws
in the largest ones—all extreme
unctions during war, when Sarah with
her mental powers scoured local battle
grounds for grievous men. Elam would
retrieve them after dark on carts, ducking
underneath the body parts blown
in trees by cannon blasts, skirting when
he could the corpses mortifying in
the standing grain and stubble.

> Mendel was an Augustinian friar at the St. Thomas Abbey in Brno in Austria-Hungary, where later in his career he became Abbott. In building upon Elam's and Sarah's work with plants, he also set up an experimental garden, and pursued questions of biological inheritance: how traits of parental plants (seed shape, flower color, etc.) are conveyed to offspring.

                        His days were like

The Book of Job, 7:1

        the days of a hireling. On occasion, as
        his spirits shredded, he would harvest larvae
        off of soldiers swollen up and bursting
        as he held his breath, and scraped them squirming

Patented in 1858.

        into Mason jars. He seldom gagged
        like Sarah, purging what she heard of agony.

Maggots only eat dead meat—and in doing so, cleanse the wound to allow healthy tissue to regenerate. In his contempt of death, Elam uses the agents of rot and decay to promote vitality.

        He had a therapy of sorts with maggots
        to debride old wounds, and thus prepared
        beyond the destiny of dying men
        the ageless human tumble into hope—
        fearfully made, of course,
                        of which was born,
        afterwards, when the time came,
        for Elam as for Sarah, their resolve
        to immigrate with children to the foreign
        city of defeat,
                      blend with Brenda,
        hide with Arie in the ordinary
        life of men kissing women, women
        tending men amid the reconstruction
        chaos, as luminous as home.

SIRENS

BRENDA ROUND and precious was beclouded
by the animals, and made her way
into the darker parts of Elam's mutant
garden, when she could escape, to watch
the lion plants feast. Beclouded, I was
about to say beguiled, inspirited,
beset, it seems to me, by fretful speculation
at the time when Alfred first beheld
her, round and precious, in the civet vines,
naked as a maiden, green and sorcerous,
her cardinal place unshaven, her paradigms
displayed unto her gaping nephew in
the year the Lusitania sank. He
undressed himself. The sun that lit perfection
now lit him as, in the midst of revelation,
he was waving with his shirt to cover
up iniquities, and bring her back
from lions to the gallery at home,
where she was caged.
     But Arie intervened,
and with a boom of disapproval drove
her sister with a willow switch into
the creek to bathe her. Brenda daubed herself
with excrement, and needed washing. Arie
would have said, and often did in different
company, as with sopranos of
the Raleigh Baptist Women's Choir of Jewels,
among whose saints she sang, running beautifully
up the scales toward mercy,
       in so many
words, Arie often said that Brenda
needed cleansing in the quintessential
river purging sins and inclinations,
especially the ruinous, blue, deforming,
feral recreations of abuse.

> This is Alfred's first glimpse of her on his search. He is also the first to see her: Arie is lagging behind.
>
> The Lusitania sank in the year 1915.
>
> Micah 7:19.
>
> Arie's *boom* sounded much like the thunder occurring in *Huckleberry Finn*, mixed with the denunciations that often greeted Ted Hughes earlier in his career.
>
> Arie had a beautiful voice, and with her choir made several recordings of religious hymns, which sold well locally. On occasion she would sing the National Anthem to open minor league baseball games for the Memphis Chicks.

Brenda's early development provided continuing occasions to worry. She was equally violent to people, not just animals properly speaking. In general, her violence seemed an expression of her frustrations at failed communication, and her unpracticed sense of other living creatures having subjective experience. Plus, the registration of her own physical pain was blunted.	She burned her kitten in the oven, for example, whose yowling brought down buzzards to investigate—alerting everyone. Over the years, she blinded Arie's cattle dog, brained an emu, strangled Sarah's Brahman pullets, boiled a rabbit litter in the laundry tub of boiling sheets, and bit the last experimental pig, which festered with a staff infection. Elam put it down, in just that way of his with gentleness, secrecy, and furtive instincts.
There are brain disorders, such as autism, in which the immune system inappropriately prunes existing neurons from functioning circuits, with the resulting loss of mental capacity. Brenda appears to regress as the consequence of an auto-immune disorder.	On the whole, his mock daughter blew across his hopes, and brought them away as stubble, leaving him alight with doubt, and suffering a thousand apprehensions after Brenda, having ample mental wherewithal, started to regress, I guess at maybe three, maybe something less. She lost a word a day the way that pleasures age, loves fall away, until by sequence she was rendered into strangled silence—like an oracle, who on occasion blasts abstruse commands. Arie sketched her images of foods to eat because she couldn't speak her mind, which never clarified, or formed, or simply was profoundly only hers. Arie knew, but seldom Sarah. Elam hardly ever understood if Brenda hurt, whether she was hungry, thirsted, or preferred the venison to pork at meals, the broccoli or corn. Oats she always ate. She clearly hated cattle dogs.
All meats looked the same after Sarah over-cooked them. It didn't matter whether anyone could tell the difference between her broccoli and corn, since Brenda wouldn't touch either of them.	

As they should, summers settled on
the slopes of family work, winters circled
the chilled nursery, the potting shed,
an empty barn, autumns tossed, and turned
flat: the seasons flirted with each set
of promises, inspiring Sarah on any
given day to school the girls in logic,
and in languages, in hopes that Brenda
might prefer Muskogee Creek to English,
and announce her thoughts in sacred gutturals—
but nope, and nope. Arie taught herself
to read, and later spread the mysteries
of written words through Raleigh public schools,
where she came to work. She never would
forget the efforts Sarah took to educate
her in the kitchen as a kid amid
the whistling gladiolus and the spider
plants, nor her patience aimed at Brenda
like a target arrow: nothing penetrated.
Sarah sighed low over open
books of numbers magical and fair,
but even Arie anguished over calculus.
It fell to Elam teaching easy stats
to visit Brenda as a diver might
approach a creature underwater in
her medium below a night of strange
stars, and ponder who's inside, who's out
in the weary world. She toyed with his tactics.
Against the rain of failures slapping around,
and dampness generally resembling
despair, he communed once more with his muse—
Sarah, she of the dark eyelids, who
was critical, to begin with, captious,
fault-finding. Accordingly, he scrapped

These were magical days for Arie, who loved the time with Sarah reading books to her and Brenda. She learned to read chiefly to pursue, on her own, the imagined worlds outside her concrete experience. She was unusual in her day for enjoying Joseph A. Altsheler's *Henry Ware* series, which felt familiar. In her adulthood, she had occasion to wonder whether Elam was a ghostwriter for the novels.

The spider plants were useful in catching flies, gnats and mosquitoes, but once they grew large enough to capture Sarah's fiddler birds in webs the size of fishing nets, they had to go.

For example, a simple t-test.

We might argue that the use of statistics in science is largely to refute David Hume, who proved that inductive reasoning is illogical. At what point do we amass sufficient particulars to induce the infinite general law? Hume could find no logical answer.

The central task of science as now practiced is to determine whether there is a relationship between two phenomena. The null hypothesis states there is no such relationship, and so must be disproven if a cause is to be discovered to have an effect. The practice of science commonly takes as an axiom that causes actually are responsible for effects, that they precede the effects they are thought to cause, and so on—all of which has been called into question by philosophy, by the behavioral sciences, and by theoretical physics.

A case in point: Brenda did not register pain in such a way that it provided her with a deterrent against its causes. Having fallen off the porch, you, for instance, might stop spinning dizzily on the end of it. Brenda, however, never observed that cause/effect relationship. Learning proceeded differently in her.

his facts, and serpent proofs elusive in
the cracks of thought. Science didn't work
with Brenda. Behind her eyes, a zillion fiery
neurons glowed anew, illuminating
parallels and replicants in other
galaxies of monster worlds obeying
different laws of nature, and inhabited
by horned, autistic people scoffing publicly
at Elam with his null hypotheses.
He could have lost his mind pursuing hers
concretely with behavioral plans, rewarding
consequences, positively reinforcing
antecedents to those moments when
she paid attention—though she mainly spun
in place, and changed the angular momentum
of the spinning room, lengthening
the time until she toppled, knocking over
lamps and tables. Sarah locked away
the breakable crockery, and ministered
to Brenda's bleeding wounds, and bruises swelling
purple in the teal blue morning
once again risen through atomic
ruins in the night sky. She looked
abused on a bad day banging against
the furniture—or turned outdoors, she tumbled
off the porch. Elam saved her with
a rocking horse he fashioned up on carriage
springs, so she swayed safely through
the sage and desert landscapes of the multiverse,
where only Arie ever followed. Great
sister, trekking after errant planets
wandering through Brenda's horoscope,
so to speak, to exaggerate
the gravity of random items that
she's not supposed to get, but that she coveted

acutely, truly madly, and with unrelenting
noise: diaper pins, for instance, one
of which she stuck through Alfred's penis once,
memorably. You'll see later.
How her trinkets swept away the cosmic
mysteries I couldn't say. Her treasures
commonly were trifles, pins and sequins,
which adeptly, nonetheless, by magic
properties, led her by still waters.
Conversely, when she lost one—say she dropped
a sequin while cavorting with the rocking
horse—she was laid plainly open
to immortal horrors. She howled in bed
all day until her sister, if she could,
retrieved the pearl of Brenda's soul from in
the shadows of the valley of death. Once
more, the Beast would move away toward sleep
before he reached her room, leaving Brenda
unbound in her substrate freedom from anxiety.

No one saw her ever looking better—which,
in the haggard aftermath, advocated
for an exorcism. I'm pretty sure.
Arie was an age at church when,
velvet herself, she comforted her sister
Brenda hyperventilating on
the pew beside her, giddy, and getting dizzy
just before the coming of the Lord
inside the Eucharist. *Sit still,
Sweetie,* Arie whispered, with her premonitions
going off just about the time
that Brenda fainted singly at the feet
of Arie's favorite acolyte, bowling
over Simon Ison with the wine.
The Savior's blood had stained the chapel carpet

> It can be tempting to believe that Brenda selected her treasures from among things that were prohibited to her, but that assumes, among other things, that she made choices at all. It is equally probable that the objects suggested themselves to her. No one prohibited sequins.

> Brenda was anxious out in public, and tended to gasp for breath.

> These were the days when the family thought to normalize Brenda's introduction to the world at large, like every other child. So she attended church, when they could drag her there.

Isaiah 9:6

They were growing up together, Simon and Arie, and had ample time to appreciate each other's character.

The good Reverend later realized that he had succumbed to spiritual ambition, and resigned his commission to walk the Camino de Santiago barefoot as a pilgrimage. He converted to Catholicism, married a woman he met on the journey, who was wearing shoes, and together they returned to Mexico to found an orphanage near Rosarito in Sonora—from which Carl Sims, a high school teacher in Tustin, California, later adopted his son.

Mark 16:17-18

purple when the Baptist minister,
with government upon his shoulder, kindly
calmed the congregation, and humanely
ushered Brenda to the rectory,
out of public speculation, where
she gathered strength. Arie brought her home—
along with Simon, who was smitten by
the velvet sister dedicated to
the special lunacy of family feeling
in favor of a skin-deep beauty,
or expensive beauty, or glamor. Magic
sometimes works.
        Meanwhile, Preacher Hood
was recommending rituals that dealt
with heretics, as well as children with
invasive demons like a case of worms.
But just the worst time of year for absolution
with the harvest wanting in: hay
unmown in the golden fields, and rained on,
cotton eaten up with beetles. Family
pigs awaited slaughter when he started
with the holy water, pouring smoking
liquids from a pitcher over Brenda,
which spattered Arie, too, who cradled her,
and bleached their clothing white. He followed with
a laying on of hands, which Elam supervised,
who knew enough of fallen angels to
insist on oversight. Sarah on
her own refused to hear of snakes in any
ceremony near her daughter, and
in general, the household tone of reason
was misleading the religious folks,
foreseeing reclamation until Brenda,
voices ringing in her ears, was over-
stimulated by the rabbit sacrifices

made in place of rattle snakes, and bit
the fingers off a helpful elder when
he tried to pacify her as she thrashed
in bed. Whereupon, at the moment
of misfortune, every father of
the church agreed that expiation failed.
Vigils were in vain. The sexton fasted,
but regained his deadly bulk. No
relief was found in prayer, leaving darkness
inside Brenda—though Sarah saw, as she
declared to Elam, that the mice were finally
conjured from her flour barrel.

> Elam tried to stitch them back on, but with middling success, since there appeared to be something in Brenda's saliva that encouraged infection, either by suppressing immune function, or constricting the capillaries.
>
> The lack of mice at that time was a mere coincidence.

                    Around
this time, upon the downfall of the deacons
to deny the fiend, the Raleigh Baptist
women rallied in the alchemy
of common kindness, which wasn't lost on Elam,
and ministered with custard pies and tarts,
berry pies, pecan bars and sandies,
pound cakes, swirling caramel puddings,
cinnamon hearts, divinity, and many
fruit breads used to sweeten temperaments,
temper dispositions, and find occasions
for the sacrament of social meals,
serving empathy. Brenda ate
the puddings, but the point was otherwise
to bolster Sarah with the sufferance
of children, and buttress sister Arie more
than anyone, who inherited
her place on earth. Elam huddled with
his haunted truths about inhuman nature,
none of which would Arie ever recognize,
who lived with what he'd done. *Regret the past,*
he'd tell himself on days when Brenda, in

> Of course, there were also peach pies in the mix, and the recipe for one of them later found its way into the movie *Young Mister Lincoln,* in which Henry Fonda as Abe Lincoln stands on stage judging a huge slice of Mrs. Letha Perry's peach pie, along with someone's nondescript apple. Fonda pretends he can't make his mind up which is best, but he is just acting a part. Everybody else is certain.
>
> Arie never conceded there was anything different about Brenda.

It may be hard
for some of you
to think of Elam
making mistakes,
but that is how
science progresses.

Precisely the sort
of behavior for
which the Sun
God destroyed the
sailing men
of Ithaka.

her adolescence, stormed around the garden
to molest the geese, and agitated
science when she disregarded methods
meant to keep her safe. Instead, she hunted
after Elam's excess—places where
he stabled his mistakes, which engaged
her morbid powers. She found one day the hidden
manger where he fed his minotaur,
and watched it servicing a herd of shambling
cattle. He kept a zombie dog preserved
in shadows that she helped decay. At times
transparent serpents entertained her when
they strangled things, though her favorites were
the Serengeti lion plants, whose massive
voices she could duplicate. The house
would shake.

Bartletts's cousins,
Ricky and Brian
Haden.

Ovid tells of
Philomela, who
was raped by
Tereus, who then
cut out her tongue
to prevent her
from telling about
it. She had no
articulate voice;
nor does Brenda.

Brenda's
developmental
timeline appears
to be roughly
twice that of other
children.

    I know exactly what you two
are thinking, which occurred to Sarah first,
remembering forever how the randy
village men went prowling after innocence,
and hit on Lillian in the wilderness
with her heart of wrath. Occurring now
against the civilizing prudery
of Christian sin were savage noises rising
in the chest of someone otherwise
unable to complain. Violence
was free. Brenda for a second time
transformed, as do we all, her genes unzipping
to amend again into a nubile
puberty arriving late, but with
the full electric promise of erotic
drama. She was gorgeous, and immodest,
with the vocal cords of primal thought.
She'd come out into the yard, and shock

the world with a word of love in decibels
exhilarating feral cats for miles,
and deafening Sarah near at hand. She
was clueless through her teens and longer, even
after Arie married, but luminous,
igniting helpless passions, and in self-
defense would burn the retinas of heedless
men who stared unchaperoned to memorize
her lines of evidence. They lived to have
regrets and lamentations, and later many
would remember Brenda, when last seen,
as the angel of illusion opening
her brooding, bright wings to spread confusion.
Around her, loyalties loosened. Goat-eyed men,
as always, torched their friends, and brothers battled.
Suitors sweet on Arie, in the way
of things, cooled, and grew bewildered by
the jungle beauty weaving chicken bones
into her hair. Whatever for. She
was definitely haunting, her legs as long
as rainbows, leaving Arie to despair
of booted men pursuing figments through
her kitchen, angling for the lovely bubble,
lust.
    Never you worry, Elam soothed
his sobbing younger daughter. With the strength
he had, which nearly did him in, he drowned
his books, and put up bars across the gallery
to cage his elder bombshell out of memory,
away from risk—hers first, but everyone's.
Redeemed from trouble, gathered in from the lands,
Brenda didn't miss her liberties,
as when the window clears on all possible
versions of the world, disclosing here,
by luck, the prince of the power of the air

She was the spitting image of Monica Bellucci at 18 years old—which was a torment to her parents, and most of Shelby County.

A retina can be burned by prolonged exposure to a bright source of illuminating radiation—which if causing a burn will commonly affect the macular area. The nature of the injury is photochemical, rather than thermal damage.

There were those primitive souls who were goaded all the more by the chicken bones.

The rainbow line is from a Mozart aria, translated from the German by a pianist I met one afternoon at LuLu Carpenter's on Pacific Avenue, in Santa Cruz, California.

Elam was especially aggravated that he had to hide his child, wholly innocent, away from sexual predators.

Ephesians 2:2

We understand so little about what goes on inside her mind: what she sees when she looks at the world around her, how she makes significance, what the sources are of her fears. Except dogs. We know she is afraid of dogs.	staring in. She was menaced. Behind him, see his legions. Loose, twilight unkindnesses of ravens wheel. Vermin soldiers cross her mind. Close the door. The caterpillar men were inching in. Elam ageless as he was, in the midst of chaos, as in the loud, resounding sea, stood his ground against misrule, and spoke through his prophets writing service
Eventually, for reasons yet to be disclosed, Sarah and Elam applied for state services for Brenda, who was packed off, first into a hospital, and later into a group home staffed by behavioral specialists, who wrote up treatment objectives that, in Brenda's case, included that she not kill anybody.	plans. Brenda over many years inhabited the gallery and inner rooms by day. By night she'd walk with Elam through his pilgrim garden, calling to the lions rooted in their pride by the umbilicus that tethered each to each, and all into a private history. Every morning, Arie cooked her sister oats and puddings, until Simon Ison called her off into her marriage bed.
Keats was there among the group: he had trained as an apothecary and surgeon, before he devoted himself to his poetry.	Sarah had by then been off into the afterlife conferring with the dead apothecaries on their formulas for drowsy numbness, and the drains of sleep. She huddled with hundreds of the grateful ghosts, sick for home, who joined her in the woodlot, in weak light, pulling herbs with molecules creating peace chemically. No opiates, too addictive, but they hit upon
Sarah with her apothecaries found a family of bioactive compounds that can include Thorazine and Lithium.	a ring of phenothiazines and sulphur, which on even mornings, once the jet of evening dissipated, Sarah spooned into Brenda's waiting mouth, like a bird's. No question, the solution was sedating. Brenda ceased her midnight rocking,

her senses sank, she was tractable,
and snowed.
              And in this way months later,
her complexion dimmed, she attended
Arie's baby shower, fattened up,
and grabbing onto Sarah's arm, off
and on, to steady her commuted soul.
She slid into the Morris chair as if
she'd never been away, and slept the afternoon,
missing packages and sweets. Simon
cast an afghan over her, noting
nothing wonderful would come from such
obtundity—and thereby pulled the petals
of domestic harmony unwittingly,
but utterly, off. Sarah started on
about the cruelties of unrelenting
dread, misgivings, evil nervousness,
in contrast, the clemency of rest,
                    when Arie
with her old voice, swollen ankles
and everything complained about the inhumane
restraint, the changed nature, dead spirit,
weight gain, and the ungainly gait
afflicting Brenda's grace. She had more
to say, except her water broke, pouring
down its power which, by sequent steps,
through anguished labor, pared a conscious piece
of nature from the quantum sentience,
and introduced him, breathing in the words
of the world breathed out around him. Perfect.
Simon named him Alfred, after elven
counsel, which never could explain the man
we knew, you and me, who owed us hundreds
that he borrowed over years of hair-brained
schemes, betting everything on slow

The medication crystallized around the mouth of the jar, looking for all the world like rocks of sugar. Sweet crystals of balm. Sarah needed pliers to twist the lid off.

The drug had side effects of course, which is to say it had many bioactive operations, some desired (therapeutic uses), and many unwished for (side effects).

Sarah's argument is pertinent: why let a person suffer when something can be done about it?

Arie's response points out that no intervention is without consequences, and those of Sarah's medication also cause suffering. So which condition is worse?

Loop quantum gravity suggests that the world is an event, like a kiss, and that conscious perception is the agent by which one event is made out of the infinite soup of possible events.
   The theory suited Alfred, who loved the transitory chances of the real.

horses.

>	Anyway, Sarah, always sensitive about defeat, started tapering her medicines, so Brenda easily within a year resumed her radiance, and awful growling speech. She was expressive, for sure, like a gnostic goddess. Also episodically deranged again, breaking things: Sarah's middle fingers went—re-knitting, though, in minutes,

>>	absolutely unlike Alfred, skewered with a diaper pin, the way I heard it, which derailed his toileting, and plundered at an early age his moral innocence. Sarah wrapped him up in rosemary, keeping with the old ways, but her poultices went overboard, and dyed indelibly his glans and foreskin green, or greenish blue, bright bluish green, thereby threatening his future adolescence with unnatural disclosures when, inciting Brenda's instincts, he flashed his neon dick.

>>		Little did they know. Venus, Cupid, Folly. Arie had anticipated nothing on the day she slipped with Alfred, bandaged like a sandwich, back into the dairy house with Sarah there, and Elam for their help in rearing up her skittish kid. By then she was dependent, salted rightly by the sorrows of her loneliness. Fretted by the glow of ready money, Simon

The truth was, despite the obvious drawbacks, everyone preferred Brenda when she was actively beautiful.

Sarah was not one to complain, but Alfred had a grievance.

Rosemary acts as an anti-oxidizing and anti-inflammatory agent, and can enhance memory as well. The herb is also used as a natural dye.

Arie moved back into the family home on the Willow Brook Dairy since Simon's military pay was insufficient to keep two separate households afloat— his in Japan, and Arie's in Raleigh. See below.

had enlisted in the Navy, where
they taught him martial arts against his nature—
like the world's most dynamite, deadly
grocer. He never aimed a rifle, couldn't
fight, refused tattoos, and wouldn't kill
the enemy, which nearly rendered him
unsafe for naval life, until they found
his knack for languages. He was writing
home in Japanese in no time. No
one understood his Kanji, so he kept
his confidences when he told them he
was training as a secret frogman, using
a re-breather, and was shipped to Yokohama
under cover in the presidential
fleet that Roosevelt deployed around
the world. He lived for years in paper rooms,
and monitored the military plans
of emperors of ocean islands. Walking,
he was underwater wandering
among huge sponges

     at the time
when Arie, thinking like a sailor's wife,
penned up Alfred on the gallery,
with Brenda making lion noises rocking
in her altered solitude. They say
to see across the rostral surfaces
of Brenda's goddess face the registration
of a daily chore, a bath, a dinner
plate to clear, spilled salt, every
hateful imperfection of an outer
world—all such instilled in Alfred early
on the urge to please his perfect aunt,
pacifying her distress. If Arie
cleaned her up and kept her fed, Alfred touched her

He was a good swimmer, though, and saved a man from drowning in the Gulf of Mexico when he and Arie were on their honeymoon in Biloxi, Mississippi.

From December, 1907, until February, 1909, President Roosevelt's Great White Fleet journeyed around the world making courtesy calls on various oceanic nations.

 Simon Ison remained in Japan as part of an ineffective diplomatic corps, in whose service he collected information important to him, but was unimportant to his superiors. After WWII, his fine anatomical drawings and portraits in charcoal of the young Hirohito—made over three decades earlier—were discovered to express a personality and resolve that foreshadowed his decision to enter war with the United States for control over Pacific Islands.

Of course she took away the beads: she and everyone except Alfred had already learned to keep such small items from Brenda's delight. They were simply too hard to find once she lost them.

The Brother's War is the designation often used among Southern families to identify what most folks now call the Civil War. To emphasize the brothers is to recognize the personal nature of conflicts and divisions. The war was Cain and Abel written across the national landscape.

Ooh, here we go.

Of the five kingdoms of risk Alfred entertains, he was himself the origin of the most dangerous.

with invention, a dean of little men. He brought
her beads, which Sarah took away, keys,
blocks that Elam made, teeth of the great
bear he found around the killer bees
in their hives. He left her with a knife she jabbed
into her thigh, and terrified him. Other
sacrifices weren't as sharp. He gave
her Sarah's feathers from the angels in
the afterlife: they kept her up at night.
He led her to the woodlot looking after
relics from the Brothers' War. He brought
her bullets. He was after her regard,
apostolic and severe, and trimmed
her fingernails into the quick, which
would loosen her affections. You wouldn't think
so, but she let him hold her hands, and with
his scissors stimulate receptors close
to pleasure. He felt the beds of her fingers
bleed.

    He felt at fourteen old as earth
in his hormonal wash, sweet but cursed.
When Brenda would elope, often toward
the lions' den, the big cats howling in heat,
he followed as a horse, a ghost of wolves,
swans in their sloughs, a fire, to catch her masturbating
in the darker parts of Elam's woods,
with enormous risks rising around
her, and him, like dragonflies the size of raptors
rising on the plumes of heat. He was
enraptured by her fingers dipping in,
her frantic animation. She would lie
there half-asleep sometimes, untroubled by
the insect of his fascination moving
over every inch of her to reach
her entrance.

> Alfred, on the other hand,
> over intervening months, contracted
> viral meningitis, and next malaria,
> which contributed to criminal
> hallucinations and eternal visions
> of his naked, ripened aunt. He lost
> weight while in the grip of wanton optimism.
> When he stalked her through a stand of poison
> oak, he blossomed into blue-green blisters
> on his dick, which drove him out of cover,
> all his plumage in his hand, which Brenda
> noticed for the colors, and the soul
> of love erupting over her. She'd be
> the death of him, he swore it, when he pushed
> into the snarls of her terminal hair,
> losing his restraint. She fought him with
> the instinct of a tameless fox until
> he learned to turn her over on her hands
> and knees, and enter like a thief, a strange
> friend from the beginning of the world,
> a dove lost at sea. As a bull,
> he plowed into the surf, glistening.
> He was in position. Among promiscuous
> forms of his approach were unavoidable
> repetitions. Over time, overthrown,
> sprawled amid the opening violets
> and celery blooms, he grew attentive, since
> she bit him when he finished first. These
> were cruel incentives coming from his muse.
> Avoiding havoc and discovery,
> he hid his wounds at home, which threatened sepsis
> finally, and pathetic martyrdom,
> until across the ulcers of erotic
> love he smeared a salve of moly roots
> that Sarah made, to cure his heart.

Bartlett learned of Alfred's childhood illnesses by researching old hospital records. Viral meningitis is more common, and less severe, than the bacterial inflammation. Malaria is mosquito-born, and both illnesses were contracted while Alfred busied himself in the undergrowth watching Brenda.

It is fair to think of Arachne's tapestry depicting the many guises Zeus took during his frequent rapes of human women—with which Arachne won her competition with Athena, but lost her own beguiling sexual form.

Moly is the herb from which Athena concocted a potion for Odysseus, so that he might resist the effects of Circe's transformative erotic power.

	Those
Freud published *The Interpretation of Dreams* in 1899, *Beyond the Pleasure Principle* in 1920, *The Ego and the Id* in 1923, *Civilization and its Discontents* in 1930.	were times when Sarah studied psychoanalytic thought by mail, and failed to notice changes in behaviors all around her. Then, at breakfast, Elam with his shrouded insight mused about the lack of unicorns, which used to pester Brenda if she let them. They had disappeared from in the garden, leaving silver oats and bales of golden hay untouched. The symbolism damaged
Dreams issuing through the Gates of Horn are true. They are those that are fulfilled. Hence Sarah's panic.	Sarah's mental camouflage. She followed darkness none too gently through the gates of horn into the maiden territory of catastrophe, where Alfred in eclipse with Brenda licked her nipples, and had exposed her awesome target

                                             when the first

Doesn't prudence feel like that: an elderly man stammering at temptation, an elderly woman pausing before her cautious desire? Eating stewed prunes, and sipping mineral water? No gluten?	ignorant servants of the lord of prudence sighed, in no way that he wanted ever, like discretion, like old men late rising to the bait of faithless youth. The queen of plunder entered through the roof of his delusion, looking every bit like Sarah, there when he needed her, wearing medals, and releasing counter spells, which felt at first like vengeance and recrimination.

                             Good lord,
we've all been there before, channeling
remorse, but Alfred was a Gemini,
and came unglued. He was whipped. What

No one in this family was especially keen on taking orders from anyone.	arrested him was endless separation when they shipped him off to military school, where sergeants chased him through his flashbacks

toward repentance, and the Corps of Officers.
He harbored in his memories of moving
in her. In the Carolinas, in
his barracks, he hid from the beginning, tactically,
and planned on no one going missing.

          When he
returned to Raleigh, Brenda was removed
already out of joy: doctors diagnosed
her with dementia praecox, and locked her in
a hospital away from lions, though
they let her run into their tamer garden
full of asphodel. Her nurses were
unmarried, sweetly wearing white. Sarah
vetted each. Monthly, Elam was
admitted to the unit, bringing clothes
from church, custard pies and tarts, and well
within the year he moved her rocking horse
into her peerless room.

Dementia Praecox ('premature dementia') is a psychiatric diagnosis indicating a rapid loss in early life of mental clarity, and a descent into irrational, chaotic thought. Over time, the term has been replaced by *schizophrenia,* which is in current use.

 As diagnostic formulations have improved in their scientific basis, Brenda has come to be thought autistic.

HOW THE WIDOW VELMA
LEARNED TO DANCE

UNLIKE ELAM lately, Sarah like
a river green with alligators acted
dangerous and patient, with her secrets
waiting to be wrestled from her elements
and bare obsessions,
                    where I was trying, by
the way, not to look, or if I did,
not to stare too carefully. I
had never heard of Brenda until I
returned to Raleigh after my hiatus—
and against my principles, it followed
that my curiosity was charmed
and chased through retrospections, tromping through
their memories one prescient afternoon
when we were packing up the house. Partially
in disbelief, I heaved incredibly
the crates onto the porch, sorted skeptically
through Velma's loving cups, labeled in
a quandary all those crazy videos
that Nate had made of Alfred's funeral,
taping Brother Cole's oration at
the graveside, teary eulogies, wailing
and convulsive weeping when we lowered
Alfred in his coffin in the ground.
Someone say *Amen*.
                Possibly
you knew already how the high-roofed
house had come to chaos. I was uninformed
myself, but not offended, really, stunned,
though, now that Elam was persuaded
they should ditch the Raleigh Baptists, the town
itself of Raleigh, and Tennessee entirely
with its pessimists—Sarah's been
insistent—and transport themselves instead
to Santa Cruz among the sea kings,

In her later years, Velma was a celebrated ballroom dancer, and renowned, though not respected, within the family for her disregard of proprieties more suitable to her age, and to their taste.

For details, see Chapter 2 in *Genealogies*.

Bartlett arrived from his foreign travels on June 22, 1982. When he met with Elam and Sarah, he discovered they had decided to move their household, and was recruited to help with the packing—which they finished on June 24th, just before the movers were to arrive.

In 1885, three Hawaiian princes visited Santa Cruz and, after carving boards from native redwood, taught the locals how to surf.

The garden has largely reverted to native plants, or native invasive plants, like kudzu.
The largest seeds were those to his flying horses, which he could no longer germinate because the pollen was sterile—smoked by that disastrous nursery fire.

Maudy is twelve at this telling, playing the *Two- and Three-Part Inventions*, which are a collection of thirty short keyboard compositions that Bach wrote as exercises for his students—which are, nonetheless, gorgeous.

A recent study at the Harvard School of Public Health has determined that the daily consumption of three to five cups of coffee decreased risk of mortality by 15%. This decrease may be offset, of course, by certain thoughtless or otherwise goading behaviors.

surfers, and the first organic farmers.
They'll fit right in, blissful.

                        But like I said,
the rooms were full of boxes, the yard unmown.
Rank with wild inceptions and the mother
of all grubs and infestations, Elam's
garden had gone to seed, some the size
of beach balls, leaving Elam on
his own to drop into nostalgia. He popped
a funeral tape, one of many, into
the VCR. They were never edited,
mere footage over days of candid takes,
which contributed to Elam's inattention
to the details later plain and inescapable.
Since Maudy in the music room was practicing
her Bach Inventions on the cheap-o leased
piano, Elam turned the volume up
as Velma fell apart again on screen,
and he was listening in on Sarah's prayer
flutes, blown with beautiful lips, when
he glimpsed a silhouette, beheld a fluky
lineation, I don't know exactly,
sighted something homeless. Even that's
not right. I heard him wheezing. Not to be trusted
were the strange thoughts running in
his mind, so when Sarah brought his coffee
in, she caught him cutting through the packing
tape to rummage after funeral
cassettes in every labeled crate. Well,
damn. He needed her to not tell
him stuff. *Help me,* he suggested, as
she stood and smoothed the apron of her blatant
aggravation. Her apron like a black
sail on the horizon of affliction.

She was good for things like packing—boxing
up a worldly place in the oldest countries
for the train of transmigration to
another power—while Elam's like the widowhood
of good sense. *Poor Baby,* Sarah
breathed, considering the curt lift
of caffeine, and skirting the debris
not exactly like a running back.
Relax.
      She sat beside him in her permanent
body, like a crowd of flowers in
the living room, thinking glad and gracious
things for his eventual apologies,
but feeling bent by the unruly moment
anyway, with the engines of
her recognition spooling up as Elam,
undistracted, forwarded the tape.
Wait, what? Elusive people scurried
on the hectic screen. *Wait.*
                       They stared
in concert at a Christian on the tool
shed, balanced on the roof beside
the angel Arie Elam Ison, there
to hover over Alfred in the naked
spirit, her wings obscuring half the torso
of another fascinating figure
in the garden in the background, hidden
in the lion plants—who threw an apple
as the camera cut to other vistas:
someone in the kitchen rolling joints,
a cameo of Osgood paying the
pianist and the dizzy trumpeter.
Elam saw himself release his winged
horses to the wild, in a final
tribute that aroused astonishment

The movers were due by the weekend. Plus she couldn't help feeling that maybe Elam was less invested in moving to Santa Cruz than she was.

For those who may be reading these lines in a distant future far from now, a running back was an offensive player in a violent game, whose primary role was to advance the ball every Sunday by running with it toward goal posts, and against defensive opposition. Often they attempted to be evasive.

He'd climbed up, enraptured by a live angel, and was nearly brought to heaven when her wings brushed him off the roof, shattering his nape-nerve. He survived his visionary trials and, after physical therapy, worked from his wheelchair with Jimmy Carter in Habitat for Humanity.

An odd, provocative thing to do in that part of the garden, among the lions.

Possibly Wayne Jackson from The Memphis Horns—and, sadly, Phineas Newborn, Jr. on the piano, who did not thrive in Memphis.

That is, Little Rock, Arkansas, 148.8 miles west of Raleigh on I-40.

Bartlett has it now in his bedroom, on his nightstand: King James version, with Evelyn's careful notes in pencil in the margins. He has yet to remember to return it.

Alfred met these women wearing their peach skirts at the track when he played the horses.

Diana in Roman mythology is the wild maiden goddess of the hunt. Persephone is a vegetation goddess. She was abducted by Hades into the Underworld, where she remains for 6 months each year, corresponding to the pomegranate seeds she ate at his table. As the Queen of Hades, she visits the curses of living people upon their souls in death. She returns to earth each Spring, renewing the mysteries of fertility. Don't mess with her.

A weapons-grade substance is pure and essential in its qualities. | among poetic souls as far away
as Little Rock. Soon they saw where Evelyn
set her Bible down and never found
again, and once they noticed Nate was focusing
on sketchy women with their goddess hair
and wearing clogs, or peach skirts and costume
pearls. So they despaired of finding who
was throwing discord in the form of apples
in the garden,
         when the camera panned
across the public mob of Raleigh churchmen
to a hothouse beauty just emerging
from the nursery. Right there.
She was dirty—but transcendent, like
Diana hounding after deer, like
Persephone rising baffled from the winter
earth, spitting seeds she'd eaten from
her lousy pomegranate. Right. She was
confusing. It could wound your heart to watch
her walk into the wood lot, her stained
lips parted. She was mammal, you
could see, her animal heat a feature of
her composition. It was worth your soul
to notice she was naked as a snake
beneath her camisole, and in her linen
slacks.
    She always got away, was Sarah's
thought out loud. How she knew escaped
me at the time—or why, in front of weapons-
grade loveliness and bloom, Elam
was unmoved. *Here's the cause of thunder,*
I was thinking as they cued the tapes
the way, as sailors, they had charted reefs
and hidden sills of rocks around the spines
of silent islands full of spices—as if, |

I mean, a life lay in the balance, or
a misadventure. I sat breathlessly
behind them undetected, where I formed
my theories who the goddess was, or elemental
mortal. She looked illegal, really young,
depending on the angle at this distance
as she disappeared into the woodlot
out of recollection, evidently.
She ambled into subtlety as Alfred
was ascending, staring sadly after
her alluring back before he turned
with Arie into light. He wasn't willing,
I could tell, though he was also hearing—
who could not?—the widow Velma bellowing
like raging surf. She disturbed the peace
of mind of all departing spirits with
her grieving, plus her new infection of
regret, and in that state she galloped through
the bedroom, through the mortuary in
restraints, over days of Valium
into the graveyard to the grave, and on
the brink of panic.

                  I was on the verge
of an epiphany regarding guardians
and higher powers in the garden at
the funeral, when Elam mentioned *Brenda*
like an intervention, plunging us
therewith as counterparts into our mutual
investigation and betrayal. Sarah
in a show of heart was cursing in
the pantry in a ceremony handed
down by sailors damning fucking everything
about her portion of the story, starting
with the moment Alfred as an officer

His theories seem to hint that she was of sexual interest to someone. Hence her strategy to hide inside the nursery.

There is no reason to suppose a person, newly dead, will lose his taste for physical beauty, or become immediately insensitive to the pull of human empathy.

Bartlett admitted later that he had begun to think Brenda was an unacknowledged, illegitimate child of Alfred's.

Sarah is protective, and unhappy regarding the implicit switch to judicial rules, out of the friendlier social concept of communal illness, which allows the hope for restoration to general health.

returned from military school, and learned
how Brenda was in chains inside a mental
ward. He staggered, lost his shit, and shot
at Elam, taking pains, who simply knocked
him senseless with a wagon spoke, and took
the guns. Under the atomic madness
of the night sky white as winter,
Elam, when he looked back, even
a month later, freaked, and was never
to forget his violence against
his grandson on the ground. *Jesus,* Sarah
yelled, afraid he'd killed him, which he hadn't.
Raising Alfred up from dust, he walked
him stumbling to the nursery, and fished
around for tourniquets. Over time,
the facial lesions healed, the hematomas
would resorb, and cerebellar insults
would repair like fledgling birds coordinating
whirring wings in timeless air. Balance
would restore, in short, though durable
despair deployed, which of course, in the
event, it would with Alfred disallowed
forever from the catastrophic grace
of Brenda's hot divinity, last
seen in asphodel locked away.
Until the day she killed him, he would build
on fantasies and wild invented romance
reddened by his excess.

                        Let me finish.
Destiny was lurking in the background
salting meat, when Elam thought of butchery
as reclamation, as a trade for saving
Alfred from himself. In autumn frosts,
therefore, they slaughtered pigs together, where

Side notes:

A hematoma occurs when ruptured blood vessels bleed between the separate layers of outer skin. We used to call them blood blisters.

His two cousins had started yelling at this point.

the terrified and screaming animals
were never heard again. Elam demonstrated
how to open up a case, and pare
the primal cuts and sides, dressing joints.
From scraps and gristle, grinding sausages
was awful work. Alfred, trimming belly
meat, would stab himself, or hack his hand
in half, slick with leaf fat, and bleed
like the ebbing sea onto the sawdust
floor. He was chronically anemic
by the time that Velma from New Mexico
arrived in mourning on her smoking train,
her sisters well in hand. Their mother was
tubercular in Alabama, and
removed to Clovis for the desert air,
desperate, where she asphyxiated
as expected, and was buried there
among the arrowheads. I'm told her grave
was dug by archeologists, who to
a man ignored the orphaned sisters for
the artifacts, and academic fame
around the corner.
                      At the station, having
blown the birds away, the silver train,
on schedule in a storm of oxygen
and altered carbon, broke for empty country,
leaving streaks of soot, irregular
feathers of black soot everywhere
outside, and three remaining Sargent women
thin as crows to wait for distant relatives
to come and claim them. Once the church had word,
they were retrieved, and divvied up among
their kin. Lilian was married off,
and banished into Texas with her Catholic
conductor from the train. Eartis was

A military career was unlikely for Alfred, given his continuing ineptitude with weapons, and his inability to follow orders consistently. Neither tendency troubled anybody in the family much.

The routine use of sharp implements, such as long knives and saws, renders butchers vulnerable to bleeding wounds.

Clovis, New Mexico, was a western hub for rail freight. The area is also famous as a site of prehistoric peoples, who distinguished themselves by their aesthetics in fashioning flint arrowheads—which were deadly, but also delicate in their symmetry. To some poetic minds, they resembled bits of lace made from rock.

Velma, Lilian, Eartis.

Such relatives as they had left were on their father's side of the family, who came from Memphis.

Raleigh was resolutely Baptist. Even the Black churches were Baptist. Everybody went to church, and was Baptist, except the Catholics.

Virginia Woolf in her *Diary* is eloquent about the problems of moonlight during WWI.

Eartis was of little help, bless her.

Her chicken farm was tiny by later standards of mega-farms, but she needed help nonetheless to slaughter the volume of chickens that she had. Plus she had no idea about butchering, which she needed to do properly in order to sell them to restaurants.

At one end of the Street of Parrots was the red-light district, the professionals of which took a practical interest in relationships.

She was hesitant to trade her freedoms for the inevitable marital compromises. From her point of view, marriage was a lot to put up with.

inclined to weep, which harmed her speaking voice,
and stayed with Velma early on before
the house was crowded on the chicken farm,
which they inherited or overtook,
which suited Velma, who was tough, even
upright, as when in war in cities, citizens
beneath the luminous moon outwear a nightly
rain of bombs. She carried on alone,
selling fertile eggs, until she waded
like immortal death into her chicken
arks, and culled the broilers and the unproductive
pullets. Whereupon, sensibly
as usual, she called on Alfred as
a businessman, it must have been, and spent
a week together butchering her hundred
hens or so, and every rooster but
the few she needed for the future. Feathers
blew into the brash and oleander
bushes. Mustelids like mink and weasels
crept around for organ scraps, and stepped
in traps instead. Velma sacrificed
the lot of them as well, and sold the pelts
and poultry feathers to the venders on
the Street of Parrots, where the talk was starting
up among the friendly women wearing
silver scales, and men with facial hair
about the pair of them. Alfred nursed
his bleeding heart, and as a corollary
Velma felt she'd be better off not
to starve, than not to have him under foot.
He warned of famine, in a way. From there
they could prepare for shocks and random barren
times, or heedless fire. She guided him
toward stepping out like nomads in
a desert full of moons, like phantoms

freed by Orpheus. They could see
their breath. She planted thoughts of ballroom dancing
at the Peabody Hotel, no less,
and Alfred in the process cantered like
a refugee from existential dread.
They turned on through the Starlight Room
beneath Arcturus, Polaris, whirling
on the parquet floor with elegant
misgiving giving way to confidence
and recognition of the fates. They lived
beyond their means for once, and last were seen
swinging toward a mutual accord
regarding secrets and immoral stunts,
when the evening ended with a charming
Chardonnay, on the house, its palate
bright with white flowers, ripened Asian
pears, and spiced with feminine acidity
that ages well, toasty, with a hint
of tears from an Alsatian child. Velma
metaphorically poured it on
her wounds. In sipping, Alfred tasted something
from the River Styx, disinhibiting,
and soon invulnerable to second thoughts,
in public he proposed widely as
his mercy flowed, just the way that Velma
could accept, because she had a room
of witnesses. *You know what, sure,*
she answered, pleased with her effect. And if
it all should come at her, birth and bankruptcy,
if she were offered to exchange the effigies
of her exacting life and death for different
magic, other tragedies, if
it happened that she could, she wouldn't, since
the plans were hers, the chances her constructions,
dangers shared by everyone, and her

Velma loved dancing, and one of her abiding sorrows was Alfred's total disinterest in dancing once he and she were married, despite the fact that once he was engaged in the music, he enjoyed himself.

Bartlett is referring to a 1982 Chardonnay from Beringer Vineyards, one bottle of which he sampled with a convivial criminal lawyer in Redwood City. The complexities of a good wine are a marvel.

One of the known properties of the waters of the Styx was invulnerability. Achilles' mother dipped him headlong into the river, which rendered him invulnerable—except around the heel she was holding while she dipped him. Alfred's invulnerability has led him into danger of a different nature.

Often among surviving friends and family there is a tendency to think the years that end a life appropriately sum up all the years preceding that end. We might argue that the circumstances of death cannot adequately sum up the qualities of life. Velma was only 19 when she wed. *I Corinthians*, Chapter 13, 1-13. At his wife's insistence, Alfred soon abandoned the butcher shop. Charles Albert Tindley, (1856-1933), who was born of slave parents. Alfred A. Ison and Velma Sargent Ison. Here was their one and only attempt to hire someone to help them out on the farm, which did not end well. Alfred was the one who found him, and noted the steam.	rewards were savory. So if we're ever weary with foreknowledge, just remember her resolve. Attended by the gods of modern love, she readied for the wedding Sarah least of all expected, and therefore no one could forget. Alfred bought a dapper suit. Velma crammed her youthful spirits narrowly into the dressy empire silhouette her mother wore before her, also gorgeously, among her maiden friends. Once upon a time, the Reverend Wardlaw opened to *Corinthians*, and spoke in the tongue of angels. Charity removed a mountain. Now hush. Watch. On the altar, Alfred with his bandaged hand, dropped the ring. Velma caught it deftly in her cuff, and made a vow. Now if ever was the time to kiss. The Choir of Jewels sang their sacred music, belting out a Tindley ballad while the wedding couple stepped like primal dancers down the steps into unbridled sun, climbed around the flower-hung horses, and were carted off in the direction of the universe of chickens—small-brained beasts with which they made a living on their farm, known as Ison Chickens ever after. They hired a man to help with chores, good with horses, and even though a lightning blast would later in the year, in the pasture, burn his chest-bones black, and boil his inner liquids, so ungodly columns of his steaming lymph were whistling, curling from

his inner ears, yet earlier today
he was alive to chances for an extra
gesture, and unhitched the horses, letting
Alfred carry Velma through a threshold
into married license.
      I doubt if Velma,
when the time came, noticed his
tattoos, she wouldn't look,
        and after disappointments,
Alfred from the Grange brought a book
on breeding horses home, which, granted, was
an education, but likewise terrifying,
what with diagrams of massive penetration
and the rest. Let it be said that Velma
never by analogy identified
with horses, never tied her nature to
a mare in heat, and subsequently in
her narrow bed, she turned away from pleasures
that would measure her among the beasts.
She carried on until conceiving Evelyn
within the year, then let gestation separate
her from the earth, every morning rising
allied with the Holy Family,
not immaculate, but not repeated
either. Correlated. Gravid with
her glory, she was multiplied in sorrow
and conception, spotting early in
her first trimester, which resolved, but followed
with incontinence, then constipation,
cramping and contractions. Vessels in
her upper legs were braided into bluish
knots and snarls. She felt firsthand the power
of the Lord, who swore in Scripture to
oppress prolific women with a woeful
labor,

During a sudden summer thunderstorm, Mr. Battle Mosely III sought shelter underneath the solitary chestnut tree out in the pasture, where he had been forking hay for the horses, when lightning found him.
 Alfred cut down the tree, which he considered a danger to man and beast, and once the wood was milled, he made an armoire from it, in which Evelyn now hangs her lingerie and robes.

In the Christian tradition, this would be Mary and Joseph, in the manger.

School systems at the time commonly disallowed married women to be employed as schoolteachers. If women married during their employment, they were required to leave. Consequently the depth of ignorance among all students regarding multiple subject matters remained preserved.

Genesis, Chapter 3: 16.

In this she was
as heroic as any
Arthurian knight,
Gawain for instance,
at the Green Chapel.

Nina was her midwife
here, an aesthete, who
was in her practice
largely so she could
watch the colors
bloom as the newborn
baby started breathing,
and turning pink.
Exactly like a sunrise, she
often thought.

He was smoking Old
Golds at the time, but
quit upon Evelyn's
birth.

Everyone was trying to
promote the illusion
that childbirth was
unremarkable—or at
least keep the truth
among the women
alone.

If given the chance,
the vegetable world
will redeem the earth,
absorbing carbon
dioxide from the air
to combine with water
and light, and form
carbohydrates. They
respire oxygen in its
place.

so when she was delivered, grunting,
from maneuvers no magic could enchant,
she was perfected in religion, as if
her cells were all replaced at once, and she
was new as Evelyn, messy at
her breast, but pinking up—whose voice was as
the roar of multitudes in Alfred's ears,
once he was allowed inside. As when
in deep-sea sailing I would see
the morning ocean hush ruffled by
a weak wind stirring over the blue
surface, and fathoms blackened beneath it, so
when Alfred entered were the women moved
to make adjustments to his cloud of smoke,
and nicotine that stained his fingers from
unfiltered cigarettes, which the midwife
washed with water doctored with a bit
of iodine. The bloody sheets were wadded
in a corner, Velma rendered modest
by a gown, Evelyn washed and swaddled
in the patience of a plant emitting
oxygen, a baby evergreen
bedecked with ornaments—the beryl films
of fingernails, pearls of her perfect
corneas, through which she stared at Alfred
and beheld the open macrocosm
of devotion. Total adoration.
He was wholly unprepared for what
was made. With a cleaned-up fingertip,
he cleaned the coral whorls of her ear,
and let her sleep against him while he wept
amazed. Velma slept, exhausted. Other
country women cleaned and took the laundry,
leaving Alfred in the room of his
own keeping, where he breathed with Evelyn

in honesty, as it always shall be.

She was born like this. Thinking back,
when did either of you ever hear of Alfred
anything but his unfailing self
with Evelyn? When I mentioned his
devotion, what I meant was how he scooped
his daughter from the start into an interval,
a model of their own, hermetic, more like
a city they comprised of momentary
presences together over years
in daily sequence, unconditional
allegiance like a team of songbirds,
small-winged, comfortable together,
in the field or mowing, feeding. She taught
him complicated narratives about
commitment. He let her drive the tractor, clearing
the way before her. She with unrecoverable
innocence invested in her gentle
dreams. He would offend her enemies,
and brained a rooster famous on the outhouse
roof that flew at her. With pardonable shyness,
she grew up to leave him,
                                      while Velma all
along was laboring to save the farm.
The barn was burned, uninsured, though Alfred
managed to release the Barbary mare
and foal into the archetypal field
of sugar beets. When disease advanced
among the chickens, wiping all but one
away with a contagious parasite,
Velma wrung its neck to let the economic
wreck continue its perfection. That
was when she sold the land, and went to work
for Mrs. Usdan fitting spectacles

Whatever else that Alfred was, he loved being a father. No faults to find there.

They had a 1928 John Deere Model GP. Osgood now owns it, in fine running order. You can't kill a good tractor.

In 1940, the Ison's were among the first farm families in Raleigh to have indoor plumbing installed in their farmhouse. The innovation was popular, but expensive.

You might think that this lone chicken represented the future, since it was resistant to diseases, but Velma was done with farming.

Everyone in the family bought their glasses from Mrs. Usdan's optometry shop, where Velma told them what to wear. Later in the century, the family was an inspiration to the young Gary Larson on one of his cross-country excursions through the Deep South.

Brenda was moved out of the Tennessee Home and Training School for Feeble-Minded Persons in June, 1968, and into a community house built in Whitehaven, near Elvis Presley's Graceland. She had four roommates, and the home was staffed 24/7, commonly by African American women who maintained the home, and cared for the residents. The move was part of a program of deinstitutionalization as a way to cut government budgets. No one really wanted to pay for the mentally ill.

and selling hearing aids. With an admonished
spirit, Alfred kept the books for Willow Brook
and other dairies, nothing in it but
the minuscule predacious sharks of boredom
ravening his mental peace. Evelyn
was married off, and entering the little
heaven of her nest. Velma was
professional, and anyway had spent
the decades deadened by her work, washing
up with cold water. Neither one
of them could even then remember an
emergency arising ever out
of Alfred's attributes, covered by
the golden labor of their memories,
which were incomplete historically,
sadly,
    so when he started up with Brenda
innocently in his own mind
of midnight waterfalls, visiting
on weekends at the structured home she lived
in with her supervision, all untrained,
no one had complete elucidation
of the traps and passages before
a grinning nephew calling on his favored
aunt, autistic, unpredictable,
and natively as rubious as Leda,
Queen of Swans. Staff would dress her like
a heavy wind in cast-off rags to blunt
the force of her appearance, but Alfred often
bought her better clothing, leather sandals
for her winged feet, accessories,
then brought her like a magic wand for barbeque.
She was sensational, turning heads,
so that if we were to see a light flaring,
such as that burning in a beacon

flaming on a formidable coast, that light
would look like Brenda beckoning for second
helpings with the manners of a famished
galley slave. Patrons would remember
the penumbra of her streaming hair,
the Mikimoto pearls, her beads of perspiration
as she spewed the contents of her greasy
meal inside of Alfred's just-washed
truck. Tell me that's not cosmic
as it fell to Alfred how to clean
her up with hoses at the car wash curving
as soon as not into the euphemism
of his joy. He toweled her off, changed
her into summer muslins, then drove her home,
abashed and belted there beside him
like a felony. She was key.
He'd touched the signal body of adrenalin,
and Lust, his endless friend, was riding in
the back, corpulent, with her colossal
arms around his neck.
                Thinking like
an animal, he wanted Brenda at
the Memphis Zoo, where she tempted the
Americans, alike with foreign visitors,
by calling to the lions in their native
language, deafening the local *homo
sapiens,* and panicking okapi
and perceptive buffalo. She was
exciting riots. She'd rise sometimes, like nothing
you have ever seen, unless she's like
a sister creature, rising up against
the cages full of masked, flapping vultures,
raptors and exterminating angels
she was agitating. Alfred for
the public good, determined they should hoof

Alfred took her once to Justine's, but more often to Jim's Place on Shelby Oaks Drive in East Memphis.

The particular women staffing Brenda's house were wise and sophisticated in the predatory ways of men in general around disabled women, but especially white men, so Brenda was chiefly dressed in camouflage as a means of protection, which she sorely needed.

Alfred was able to pay for Brenda's clothes out of his monthly operating budget, and from his occasional winnings at the racetrack, but he had to embezzle money from the Willow Brook account to buy the pearls. With that said, he had almost repaid all the money before he died untimely. He never managed to repay what he borrowed from time to time from Bartlett, and from Ricky and Brian Haden.

This zoo is not particularly large, but it is popular there to feed the giraffes with their long purple tongues looping down for crackers.

This would be the Hernando de Soto Bridge. The design is a continuous through arch, with bedstead end posts. It can't compare to the Golden Gate Bridge, but it's pretty enough.

A mare may not reliably display signs of estrus. To determine whether she is in season, the mare is 'teased' by leading a stallion up and down the outside perimeter of her paddock to see whether she comes forward and demonstrates the classic signs of interest.

Surgeons, even animal surgeons, are a brand of sociopath who exercise their violence toward others in socially sanctioned circumstances—and therefore get away with it.

What is there to say?

it out of sight forever, exiting
on Prentiss down to Poplar going west,
and weaving on the back roads to the Bridge,
across, and into Southland Park,
       where he
was friendly with Security, and crucially
with farriers and grooms, horse trainers,
jockeys, thoroughbreds in stalls, the teasing
mares, and jealous women once they looked
at Brenda with her elements. At
the stables, handlers in the hay loft placed
their bets on Alfred, same as ever, steering
Brenda toward the jumpy colts. Nearby,
mares were whickering advice. *Which
is none of the worse,* he thought. Their voices were
a thread of gorgeous, useless noises carried
in the summer air of his imagination.
Looking back, we know the track was his
preferred oasis and escape. With Brenda
on his arm, he greeted veterinarians
still buzzed by bloody surgeries. *Feel
my biceps,* he would say, and introduce
her to the geldings standing placid in
their harnesses. She fed them golden apples.
No one paused, or would condemn him when
he exercised her in the paddock, on
the spreading hay in vacant stalls, in
his truck bed beneath a turnout blanket,
anywhere in sympathy and what
she let him touch. He was never rough.
He sighed, and wouldn't sleep until his mind
was lost.
    Brenda, on the other hand,
unmade the universe. Ostlers later
would recall, for instance, just to pick

an incident, the use she made of whips
when she was inconsolable, and nearly
flayed her naked heavy-laden nephew
pressing near, his hormones huge in him.
She caught him undefended. He got used
to it: some unexpected hidden curtain
opened in her heart, and chaos exited
to look around. He was close. Her violence
was rushing past the other random men
admiring her, and only hit on Alfred.
Their coupling was powerful. Even
she was stretched by Alfred's prehistoric
pressure fingering her self-restraint.
She pushed him through a window, single-paned,
which added to the string of sutures he
accumulated all on her behalf,
and stitched him to his passion. No one else
was laughing, or surprised by extra burns
and sprains, but wagered as professionals
on fatal accidents and the inanities
of funeral arrangements,

      only purely
to uncover the inebriating
grief of actual disaster after
Alfred died. Odds were he was leading
tethered geldings by the breeding shed
when Brenda did her lion thing, and replicated
the original disorder of
creation, terrifying every horse
and animal, which bolted screaming, hauling
Alfred like a harrow screaming straight
as a string across a field of cotton spines
and stubble that delaminated him
by layers, an eye and orbit lost directly.

To be entirely fair, a whip is designed for abuse.

Brenda seemed to require extremes in stimulation in order to register physical sensation. Her interpretation of that sensation, when she felt it, was not linear.
 Alfred was the sort of man on whom everything seemed to register. If people were logical entities, then these two matched dialectically.

Increasingly he was undecided whether the pain of his injuries contributed to, or was a distraction from his pleasure. After a while, he didn't care.

Half his precious face was grated off
inside a minute as the runaways, in transit,
dragging Alfred at gallop, ran
like rolling breakers foaming over obstacles
and rocks, which he would hit in sequence. Once
momentum flung him sideways, he was done,
impaled at speed among the cypress stumps,
a purple rope of colon fluttering
for all the world like awful ribbon slapping
on the stubs and saplings as they happened
by. If he was howling now, he wasn't
heard. An arm was gone, a leg was severed
at the knee
                before the horses foundered
near the river in the bottomlands
across from Memphis, where the stable vets
were called to put them down. Trackers had
a job to find what Alfred lost and left
behind before the dogs and ravens ate
him raw. Elam kept an inventory
in the freezer, each of Alfred's pieces
labeled somewhere in a given space,
until they reassembled him with wire
and wax, remade his face, and laid him like
an effigy inside his coffin in
Memorial Park. The mortuary artist
caught his likeness. Jesus wept. People
green and faint would dwell on tragedy,
harp on accident, and still remain
as ignorant as sin regarding circumstance.
That's why I'm nursing my acquaintance with
the stoolies at the track, and Alfred's women
friends with numbers, who remember him,
and listened to orations at the graveside
covered in the yellow color of

The shortest verse in the King James Bible, *John*, Chapter 11: 35.

The artist, Alder Klimt, branched out in his career to make waxen statues of celebrities, and later yet sculpted attractive silicon sex dolls that were sold out of Texas.

complicit shock. One of them in boots
had kindly captured Brenda, whom the racing
vendors fed for free, and turned her loose
at the reception, near the nursery,
where she disappeared like spirits in
her native garden, and eluded great
sorrow, not for long, which the very
air in currents carried as the smell
of small mortalities. My nose was bleeding.
Velma bellowed from the bedroom, but
over time, presented with conditions,
live or die, she automatically
resumed. Her grieving and apology
abided out of view until she glided
once again like Cyd Charisse onto
the ballroom floor, and won her loving cups
and public mention when, by ancient glamour,
she reminded judges at cotillions
of their distant memories. Pairing
with imaginary partners, she
performed in rhythm her initial promises
with Alfred to be wed together, indivisible
in mind, her body otherwise suspended
like an insect in the amber music,
borne on toy horns and winds into
the working history of love.
      That's why
it's cheaper in the long run, before
the lord of mice arrives with all that
quiet, and we're silenced——why, and this
is intuition, why it's provident
to throw our open hearts unchecked at sparks
and graces, as available, amid
the race against ruthless regret. Elam's
off for Santa Cruz, where Sarah rises

Think of her relief at being returned home.

She was never as graceful as Ginger Rodgers, but had a modern, muscular athleticism. She wouldn't break your heart, but she could inflame it.

The Greek god Apollo was known as the Lord of Mice, representing music, truth, beauty, the art of healing, and the obtundity of plague.

Here is a definition of gratitude worth thinking over.

from the ocean like the muse of curling
surf herself. I have other plans.
I'm looking after Brenda. Set aside your fears.

END *of* PART TWO

BRAD CRENSHAW received both his MFA and PhD in English from the University of California, Irvine. He later obtained a second PhD in clinical psychology and neuroscience from the University of Massachusetts, where he taught neuropsychology in the graduate psychology program. For many years he worked as a neuropsychologist in a New England medical center. His poems and critical articles have appeared in various magazines, including *Chicago Review, Parnassus, Massachusetts Review, Shenandoah, The Formalist, The Sandhills Review, Illinois Quarterly, Faultline*, and others. Greenhouse Review Press published his first book, *My Gargantuan Desire*, in addition to *Memphis Shoals, Genealogies*, and a chapbook, *Limits of Resurrection*. He lives in Amherst, Massachusetts, and in Santa Cruz, California.